Comprehensive Schooling: the impossible dream?

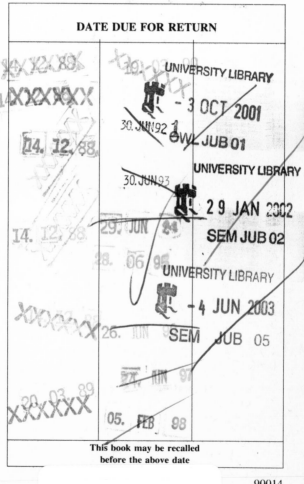
07

Comprehensive Schooling: the impossible dream?

BEVERLEY SHAW

BASIL BLACKWELL

© Beverley Shaw 1983
First published 1983

Published by
Basil Blackwell Publisher
108 Cowley Road
Oxford OX4 1JF
England

British Library Cataloguing in Publication Data

Shaw, Beverley
    Comprehensive schooling
    1. Education, Secondary – England
    2. Comprehensive high schools – England
    I. Title
    373.2'5'0942   LA635

    ISBN 0 631 13264 3 (hardback)
    ISBN 0 631 13263 5 (paperback)

Typeset in 10/11pt Palatino
by Freeman Graphic, Tonbridge
Printed in Great Britain
by Whitstable Litho Ltd., Whitstable, Kent

Contents

Preface

This book is a study of comprehensive schooling in Britain. The destruction of grammar, technical, and secondary modern schools, and their reorganisation on comprehensive lines has radically transformed secondary schooling. Great expectations were held of this reorganisation; have they been realised? I attempt to answer this question along with others relating to the principle (or theory) of comprehensive schooling itself. My own view, developed in this book, is first, that the comprehensive system has failed in practice, and second, that the theory underpinning comprehensive schooling is contradictory and incoherent.

Chapter 1 is introductory, and provides an outline of the comprehensive system in Britain more or less as it is today. I pass from a review of some criticisms of the selective system to a fuller examination in Chapter 2 of the comprehensive ideal. The rise of comprehensive schooling is chronicled in Chapter 3. The following chapter discusses the diverse pattern of the comprehensive school system, and the difficulties facing local education authorities in creating secondary schools that are truly comprehensive. Chapters 5 and 6 consider various aspects of the internal organisation of comprehensive schools: their size; curriculum; pastoral organisation; discipline; and forms of class grouping. In the penultimate chapter I discuss: the implications of comprehensive reorganisation for the future of schools' sixth forms; the notion of the comprehensive university; and the findings of research, and educational statistics, in so far as they throw light on the success or failure of comprehensive schooling. The concluding chapter summarises my views on comprehensive schooling in theory and practice, and attempts to provide an answer to that difficult question: where do we go from here?

Whilst this book expresses a view hostile to comprehensive schooling, I do not argue that in comprehensive schools all teaching and learning fails. There are many excellent teachers in comprehensive schools, and many children both enjoy their time in such schools and learn much to their advantage. Nevertheless, I do not think these happy outcomes are a consequence of the comprehensive system and principle – rather the reverse, as much good work in comprehensive schools perversely runs against the grain of such schools, and often is in flat contradiction to the comprehensive principle. I am also aware that some people adopted and advocated the comprehensive principle out of a certain generosity of spirit. Comprehensive schooling, it was believed, increased opportunities, and by breaking down social barriers of all kinds would help to make Britain a fairer and more humane society. I do not, therefore, question the good will of those who have persuasively and passionately advocated comprehensive reorganisation. Where I do find cause for concern is in a refusal to question the theory of comprehensive schooling itself, and a reluctance to look clearly at the working out of the principle in practice.

There was a time when I also refused to look too closely at what was going on in comprehensive schools; and, in my eagerness to pass on the conventional wisdom on equality and justice, I failed to note the confusions in the doctrine itself. I wish to acknowledge, therefore, and thank those comprehensive schools, and their staff, that have enabled me to see what I believe to be a truer picture of the state of affairs in our schools. I must also acknowledge my debt in writing this book to advocates of comprehensive schooling themselves, whose texts have provided much illumination on both the practice and theory of comprehensive schooling, although my response to their writings remains strictly my own. Finally, I wish to thank Mrs. Peggy Wood for her careful work in preparing this book for publication, and my wife, Angela, whose knowledge of school teaching, and unfailing common-sense, has helped me immensely in my reassessment of comprehensive schooling.

Beverley Shaw
August 1982

Chronology

1944 Education Act establishing 'secondary education for all'; but not laying down how schools were to be organised, except that there be sufficient variety so as to provide for the age, ability, and aptitude of pupils.

1945 Labour government: Ellen Wilkinson appointed Minister of Education.

1947 George Tomlinson appointed Minister of Education following death of Ellen Wilkinson. Both Tomlinson and Wilkinson were strongly opposed to the abolition of grammar schools.

1948 Middlesex LEA decided to create some comprehensive schools – in part by closing down a grammar school.

1949 Ministry of Education asked Middlesex to reconsider their plans for going comprehensive. Labour lost control in Middlesex and plans abandoned.

1951 Conservative government: Florence Horsbrugh appointed Minister of Education.

1951 The Labour Party's policy document, *Secondary Education for All*, committed the party to a policy of comprehensive reorganisation, yet equivocated on private schooling and the internal organisation of comprehensive schools. In practice, these policies were probably not acceptable to the majority of Labour Party members at that time.

1953 At the Labour Party's annual conference, the following amendment to a conference resolution was not carried: 'all fee-paying in schools will be abolished and all public and private schools will be taken over by the nation immediately Labour returns to office'.

1954 Sir David Eccles appointed Minister of Education. He was opposed to the 'assassination' of grammar schools.

1954 Kidbrooke School, the first purpose-built comprehensive, established in London.

1957 Viscount Hailsham appointed Minister of Education, replaced the same year by Geoffrey Lloyd.

1957 Leicestershire adopts two-tier system – known to insiders as the Mason–Pedley line.

1958 At the Labour Party's annual conference the following amendment to a conference resolution was not carried: that it be made 'illegal for any parents to spend any money whatsoever on the private education of their children'.

1958 Publication of Conservative government White Paper recognising the value of experiments with comprehensive schools so long as they are 'proposed on genuine educational grounds'.

1959 Crowther Report on schooling for 13–18 year olds. Sits on the fence as far as comprehensive schooling is concerned.

1960 Association for the Advancement of State Education formed in Cambridge. First of a number of pressure groups generally sympathetic to comprehensive education.

1960 Risinghill comprehensive school opens in London.

1963 Newsom Report, *Half Our Future,* on average and below average children. Reveals the limitations of some secondary modern schools in slums. Has nothing to say on the vexed question of going comprehensive.

1964 Sir Edward Boyle appointed Minister of Education. A liberal educationalist sympathetic to comprehensive schooling: so long as it did not mean the destruction of well-established grammar schools. Saw large local authority housing estates as perhaps most appropriate for comprehensive schools.

1964 Labour government: Michael Stewart appointed Secretary of State for Education. Stewart proposed the end of selection at eleven and the reorganisation of secondary schools on comprehensive lines.

1965 C. A. R. Crosland appointed Secretary of State for Education. Issues Circular 10/65 requesting LEAs to submit plans for going comprehensive.

1965 Risinghill comprehensive school closed. This closure creates controversy and comment on 'progressive' education and the comprehensive principle.

1965 Public Schools Commission established with the brief of discovering the best way of 'integrating' state and private schools. Produces a number of reports whose findings have been ignored (with the exception of the recommendation to abolish Direct Grant Schools). Crosland later revealed that the DES were sceptical of the value of the Commission.

1965 National Education Association: 'to safeguard parents' freedom of choice in secondary schooling', formed – an example of pressure group created to oppose comprehensive schooling.

1966 Ealing judgement against parents objecting to a grammar school closure. Parents argued that closure was contrary to the 1944 Education Act in so far as it diminished the LEA's capacity to provide for the age, ability and aptitude of pupils. An important judgement which eliminated a possible legal barrier to comprehensive schooling.

1967 Enfield parents secured judgement against their LEA on a minor procedural point on the issuing of notice of school closure. A loophole rapidly closed by the 1968 Education Act, reviled by some as an example of retrospective legislation.

1967 Patrick Gordon Walker appointed Secretary of State for Education.

1968 Edward Short appointed Secretary of State for Education. Former headmaster and member of the NUT. In some speeches called for the abolition of school examinations.

1970 Edward Short attempted to introduce a bill compelling comprehensivisation. Attempt failed because of some procedural confusion amongst its supporters.

1970 Conservative government: Margaret Thatcher appointed Secretary of State for Education. She issues Circular 10/70 withdrawing Circular 10/65.

1971 ILEA ceased taking up places in direct grant and independent schools: thus reducing even the very limited 'integration' between the state and the private sector.

1973 Minimum school-leaving age raised to sixteen. This had been promised in 1964 for the year 1970–71, but was delayed by the practical problems of supply. As a policy it appears to have been opposed by most teachers, though no doubt useful in terms of helping to reduce figures of juvenile unemployment.

1974 Labour government: Reginald Prentice appointed Secretary of State for Education. Prentice is later to leave the Labour Party and 'cross the floor'. At this stage, however, he is committed to comprehensive schooling. He issues Circular 4/74 reviving the policy of compulsory comprehensivisation.

1975 Fred Mulley appointed Secretary of State for Education.

1976 Shirley Williams appointed Secretary of State for Education. Later to leave the Labour Party and as one of the 'gang of four' help create the Social Democratic Party. Her political testament, *Politics are for People* (1980) reveals that she remains committed to comprehensive schooling and the abolition of fee-paying independent schools; although she is credited with equivocation on this latter issue in her successful fight in the Crosby by-election, 1981.

1976 Education Act establishing the 'comprehensive principle' that no maintained schools (with some exceptions) select by ability or aptitude. This Act abolished many LEA grammar schools – despite Prime Minister Harold Wilson's earlier promise that such schools would be abolished over his dead body.

1979 Conservative government: Mark Carlisle appointed Secretary of State for Education. 1976 Education Act repealed.

1980 Education Act: incorporating some measures from the previous administration. General intention seems to be to increase parental choice, information, and representation on schools' governing bodies. Assisted places scheme introduced in yet a further attempt to bridge the gap between state and private schooling.

1980 DES publish Macfarlane review on schooling for the 16–19 year olds. Draws attention to the problem of small school sixth forms which the review blames on falling school rolls. Has no clear policy on retaining schools' sixth forms.

1981 Sir Keith Joseph appointed Secretary of State for Education. First minister who appears positively hostile to comprehensive schooling since Margaret Thatcher.

1 Introduction

'Already in three-quarters of our schools the selective
system is a thing of the past.' Mrs Shirley Williams, 1977

Comprehensively reorganised

A major reform of the British educational system was wellnigh
completed by the early 1980s – the reorganisation on comprehensive lines of its secondary schools. This reform was begun
largely in the 1950s. The pace of change and reorganisation
quickened in the 1960s – particularly from 1964 when a Labour
government came into office after what Harold Wilson, its
enduring and egregious Prime Minister, described as 'thirteen
wasted years of Tory misrule'. The rate at which schools were
reorganised accelerated in the 1970s – even under a new Conservative administration and Mrs Margaret Thatcher, then a
tough and ambitious Secretary of State for Education, unsym-
pathetic, it might be assumed, to both comprehensive reorganisation and the egalitarian notions underpinning it.

By 1977, Mrs Shirley Williams, at that time a Labour minister
and a successor to Mrs Margaret Thatcher as Secretary of State for
Education, could declare in her Foreword to the summary of a
national debate on education carefully stage-managed by the
Department of Education and Science: 'Already in three-quarters
of our schools the selective system is a thing of the past.' (DES,
1977, p. 1). A year earlier, in 1976, an Education Act had been
passed by parliament enforcing comprehensive education and
demanding that 'education is to be provided only in schools
where the arrangements for the admission of pupils are not based
(wholly or partly) on selection by reference to ability or aptitude.'
(preamble to the Act). And although this Act was repealed by the
new-broom administration of a triumphant Margaret Thatcher,
now Prime Minister, in 1979, given the degree of local control

1

over the educational system the move towards a fully comprehensive system in Britain continued with due speed.

Social Trends 12, an official digest of statistics that outlines and
enumerates the social tendencies of the age, pointed out:

> In 1980 more than 83 per cent of secondary school children
> were attending comprehensive schools. Nine years pre-
> viously only 38 per cent were in comprehensive schools.
> Modern schools in England and Wales now cater for 7 per
> cent of secondary school pupils compared with 37 per cent in
> 1971. Grammar schools have followed a similar pattern with
> 4 per cent of secondary pupils in 1980 compared with 18 per
> cent in 1971. (1982, p. 40).

Some individuals and groups had opposed this reform. Sir Eric
James, later to become Lord James, Vice-Chancellor of York
University and chairman of a commission of inquiry into teacher
training, but in the 1950s High Master of a highly esteemed and
selective direct grant school, Manchester Grammar, had argued
that the introduction of comprehensive schooling would lead to
'grave social, educational and cultural evils' and 'may well be a
national disaster' (quoted in Rubinstein and Simon, 1973, p. 37).
But by the 1960s such condemnations were seen as reactionary
and unreasonable: showing up their proponents as 'forgotten
men' left behind in the inevitable progress towards comprehensive schooling.

How comprehensive reorganisation was opposed will be explored more fully in chapter 3; it suffices for the present to remark
that opposition in the 1960s and 70s was largely ineffectual, at
best a delaying campaign against what was seen as the inexorable
development of comprehensive schooling. Indeed the supporters of comprehensive schooling argued strongly for its in-
evitability. Caroline Benn, then Information Officer for the
National Campaign for Comprehensive Education, and Brian
Simon, Professor of Education at Leicester University, provided
in *Half Way There* an account of how far Britain's secondary
schools had gone on the road to full comprehensive reorganisation. Although Benn and Simon were clearly concerned that
the pace of reorganisation was too slow and too feebly directed
under the Labour government 1964–1970, they were eager to
point out that Britain was not alone in developing its schools
along these new lines. 'The movement towards comprehensive
education', claimed Benn and Simon, 'is not, then peculiar to
Britain alone; it is part of a worldwide movement concerned to
adapt the structure of secondary education to the new demands
of scientific, technological, social, racial, and cultural progress'

(1970, p. 13). Three years later a history of the growth of comprehensive schooling, written by Professor Simon in collaboration with David Rubinstein, a lecturer in social history at Hull University, was published in a revised edition in Routledge's Students' Library of Education: a series designed very much with a readership of student teachers in mind. (Student teachers whose numbers increased so very greatly in the 1960s and early 1970s.) The book was pointedly enough entitled: *The Evolution of the Comprehensive School, 1926–1972*. The movement towards comprehensive schooling was inevitable and evolutionary (so it was claimed); woe betide anyone who stood in the way of its progress.

It is, therefore, not surprising that the publications of the Critical Quarterly Society on aspects of schooling, and appearing regularly from 1968 under the title 'Black Paper', should have brought down upon their authors the wrath of the supporters of comprehensive schooling. The Black Papers were polemical pamphlets opposing comprehensive education and any general tendency towards progressivism in education. Five pamphlets have been published in all: the first in 1969 and the last in 1977. C. B. Cox, a professor of English at Manchester University, and A. E. Dyson, a lecturer in English at the University of East Anglia, edited the first three Black Papers. Later, the redoubtable Rhodes Boyson, a one-time headmaster and by the mid-1970s Conservative member of Parliament and front-bench spokesman on education, replaced Dyson as an editor for the two later pamphlets. In a close analysis of the first four Black Papers, Nigel Wright pointed out that: 'Of the 52 named contributors to the four pamphlets, 28 were university academics, 12 were headteachers and 8 were professional writers.' Not surprisingly, as Wright notes: 'the 52 contributors embrace a disparate range of opinions.' (p. 139.) Wright, in addition, observes that: 'The Black Papers' intention is to make a stand on behalf of the traditional standards of academic and intellectual excellence.' But his careful scrutiny of the pamphlets led him to the opinion that the Black Papers contained 'a staggering number of errors, inaccuracies and misrepresentations' (1977, p. 140).

Whatever the genuine limitations of the Black Papers they were, however, just about the only published critical literature – in the sense of disparaging and sceptical – on comprehensive reorganisation. *The Times Educational Supplement*, under an earlier editor, Walter James, had been doubtful of, if not downright hostile to, the claims of comprehensive schooling; with a new editor, Stuart Maclure, the editorial stance was a good deal more tolerant and welcoming. The 1970s saw a great many books on education published – partly in response to the market created by the development of courses on education, and the increase until well into the 1970s in the number of students training to be teachers. Many of these books were either supporting and advocating comprehensive reorganisation, or reporting upon its development in a fairly neutral and factual way.

Nevertheless, in the 1970s schooling was placed under the microscope. There was concern that standards of attainment and behaviour in schools might be falling. There was worry about what schools offer to their pupils. Were such offerings relevant either to the pupils themselves, or to what might be seen as the needs of a modern industrial society?[1] There was doubt, amongst some, that schools were doing enough to mitigate inequalities that were thought to have their origins in the family, social class, and racial differences. In many ways these worries and doubts had a perennial note about them: but a note which became louder and shriller in the 1970s. A lot depended upon the viewpoint. The perceived limitations of schooling bore some relationship to the ideological spectacles of the viewer. De-schoolers, Marxists, and the more traditionally inclined Black Paper-ites, saw schooling in very different lights, and thus- found different aspects of the school to criticise and deplore.

I have referred to the scepticism and doubts of Black Paper-ites. No doubt, as Nigel Wright observed, much in those objections revealed muddled thinking and an absence of precise and up-to-date information on comprehensive schooling. In addition, their authors were amongst those groups seemingly most likely to lose in status and esteem from the rise of the comprehensive school: grammar school teachers; university dons of an old fashioned liberal arts type who required docile students from selective schools with those skills and subject knowledge appropriate to academia.

What then is surprising and of interest, is that some of the sharpest criticism of comprehensive schooling – at least as it has been realised in practice – comes from the strongest supporters of the comprehensive principle. Professor Robin Pedley has been one of the leading advocates of comprehensive schooling. His *The Comprehensive School* was first published by Penguin in 1963; and has been reprinted very nearly every year since, and run to three editions. In Britain it is the best known presentation of the case for comprehensive schooling. His 1978 third edition was extensively rewritten, Pedley notes, 'to take account of these momentous developments [the reorganisation of secondary schooling]. . . . Its philosophy, however, remains the same.' (see Author's Note, p. 9).

Pedley in his Introduction states: 'During the thirteen years since a British government accepted the case for comprehensive secondary education, under a virtually clear sky of public and professional approval, clouds have gathered over its progress.' And he continues that 'it must be recognised that disappointment with the way it [the comprehensive principle] has been interpreted in practice is common among both parents and teachers' (p. 10). Pedley argues that: too little money is spent on schools; comprehensive schools are too big; comprehensive schools fail as community schools; there are too few mixed-ability groups in schools, and teachers ready, willing, and capable of teaching them. And what is to be condemned is 'the decision by DES and LEAs alike to describe as "comprehensive" those schools which, losing the most able children in their community to a nearby selective school (whether independent or maintained), are little more than secondary modern schools for children of average and below average ability' (p. 13). In addition, the existence of the independent schools must be questioned; '. . . a genuinely comprehensive reform cannot be completed without . . . a decision about their future role' (p. 15).

This series of criticisms – some of which, had they come from a known opponent of comprehensive schooling might have earned their author the epithet of 'reactionary'. Pedley, however, is careful to distinguish between the theory (or principle) of comprehensive schooling and its practice. It does not seem to occur to him that such a massive failure in practice (that he suggests has taken place as a consequence of 'these momentous developments') may at least demand that the principle, theory or philosophy of comprehensive education be re-examined to see if that is in any way flawed or imperfect. The points that Pedley makes in criticism of comprehensive practice will be given fuller treatment later in the book. What I wish to do here is to note the disappointment with comprehensive reorganisation expressed by one of its most capable and persuasive advocates.

Has the time now come for a more detailed examination of comprehensive education, its development and future? No doubt many people have been waiting until comprehensive reorganisation is complete before reviewing its progress. In addition, the political support that has been given to comprehensive schooling may in itself have muted criticism. Many people will have noted that comprehensive reorganisation is a part of life. Is there then very much point in questioning seriously its principles and practice? Perhaps the most sensible approach is to try to make the system work to everyone's best advantage. There is something to be said for this point of view: particularly for the busy administrator and the teacher 'at the chalk face'.

Nevertheless, there are many signs that the comprehensive school system – so recently created – is not working all that well. In addition, many supporters of comprehensive schooling are most decidedly dissatisfied with its progress. (But these are led to demand more comprehensive reorganisation not less: rather as though if one dose of medicine is not doing the trick the prescription must be repeated!) There is I believe, every good reason to examine both the system of comprehensive schooling in Britain, and the foundations on which it is built. Are these underpinnings strong enough to carry the structure erected upon them? What are the flaws in the system of comprehensive schooling? And where is comprehensive reorganisation taking us? These are the questions I hope to answer in this book.

I intend to consider both comprehensive school theory and practice. Rather more than most changes in schooling, comprehensive reorganisation has been underpinned by theory. The supporters of comprehensive schooling have never attempted to disguise this fact. Indeed, quite the contrary, for they believe that correct practice will surely follow from correct theory. That is why they have put so much importance on the articulation of the principles underpinning comprehensive schooling. Of course, it does not follow that there is unity amongst the theoreticians and a consensus on the rationale for comprehensive schooling. But to understand why schools have been reorganised on comprehensive lines, it is important to learn something of the educational, social and political outlooks of those who have supported and advocated such reorganisation. The *practice* of comprehensive schooling in Britain will be considered relative to such theorising. I will look at the politics of reorganisation; the effect of the abolition of selection; the internal organisation of comprehensive schools; the curricula of such schools; the problems that comprehensive reorganisation creates for the education and training of the 16–19 year age group; and the notion of the comprehensive university. My last chapter attempts a brief answer to that most difficult question: where do we go from here?

Supporters of comprehensive reorganisation have been fond of drawing parallels between comprehensive reorganisation in Britain and the organisation of secondary schooling in the USA and USSR. Similarities have also been found with the difficulties of going comprehensive in Western European countries. Above all, Sweden has been held up as the example for Britain to follow in creating an egalitarian and classless educational system. However, other parallels may be found somewhat closer to hand: in those policies in housing and planning conceived in the 1950s, carried out in the 1960s, and which came to an unripe maturity in the 1970s. When one considers what a desert that curious mixture of social justice, town planning, and old-fashioned cupidity has made of our major cities, it may be more than propitious to consider in some detail educational policies that paralleled those now bankrupt housing policies: more often than not condemned and abandoned by the parties and persons once so eager to support and implement them.

The comprehensive system

Let us begin our scrutiny of comprehensive schooling in Britain by giving a little more attention to the extent and pattern of comprehensive reorganisation. *Statistics of Education, 1979, Schools*, Vol. 1 (1981), records that: 'A school is classified as comprehensive when its admission arrangements are without reference to ability and aptitude' (p. xii). In 1980 in percentage terms, Scotland had the edge over Wales of children in such comprehensive schools: 96.1 per cent to the Welsh 95.5. Indeed in Scotland there are no longer any selective schools offering a six-year course – at least in the public sector. In 1971, 15.4 per cent of Welsh children were in grammar schools; in 1980 only 1.5 per cent still remained. Thus in Scotland and Wales according to the official statistics, selective schooling in the state schools is virtually 'a thing of the past'. In England, the comprehensive revolution is not quite so complete. In 1980, 81.4 per cent of children were in comprehensive schools; rather less than 4 per cent still remained in grammar schools – in percentage terms, of course, considerably less than the 18.4 per cent to be found in such schools in 1971 (when the comprehensive reform was but 'half-way there' as Benn and Simon put it). In 1980, 6.8 per cent of British children were still to be found in secondary moderns, but in percentage terms considerably less than the 37 per cent to be found there in 1971. These figures are the most up-to-date to be found at the time of writing (1982). It is unlikely that percentages in selective and modern schools will have risen since they were compiled – rather the reverse.

Of course, the figures include only children in *maintained* schools – that is schools maintained by local educational authorities (LEAs) out of rates and taxes. Such schools include the voluntary or denominational schools, such as Roman Catholic comprehensive schools, but not independent schools of one kind or another. The total number of children in independent schools is small relative to the numbers in the maintained sector. There are different judgements as to how many there are in independent schools in percentage terms: this rather depends on how this group is characterised, and of what larger population it is a percentage. For most purposes, the figure of 5 per cent probably gives a quite adequate enough impression of the size of the group relative to the numbers of children in school generally. What perhaps has to be borne in mind is that pupils in independent (or fee-paying) schools stop on at school in general longer than those in the maintained (or state) sector. We are not always comparing like with like. But however small the numbers are in such schools, they play an important part in the comprehensive school debate as we shall see.

The general conclusion is that, as far as schools maintained out of rates and taxes are concerned, Britain is comprehensively reorganised – with the larger part of the reorganisation having taken place in the 1970s. *Statistics of Education, England, 1979, Schools*, Vol. 1, records some areas not yet reorganised at that time. For example, Sutton in Greater London, in 1979, still retained 4 grammar schools and 10 secondary moderns, along with 9 comprehensive schools. Amongst the larger cities, Liverpool still then retained 10 grammar schools and 33 secondary moderns alongside 28 comprehensive schools. Bolton, in Greater Manchester, had 6 grammar schools and 19 secondary moderns in coexistence with 4 comprehensive schools. In some LEAs such grammar schools and secondary moderns are denominational schools (often Roman Catholic). Although the salaries of teachers at such schools and the greater part of the running costs (plus substantial grants toward extensions and repairs) are paid by the LEAs, a considerable degree of control rests with the governing bodies of individual schools (on which the appropriate church or denomination is well represented) or with a diocesan board: rather paralleling in function a local educational committee in its overall control of the schools within the diocesan area. Many such schools have followed the county (or LEA controlled schools) in going comprehensive, but some have not, or are rather taking their time about so doing. (Yet another area of dispute regarding comprehensive education.)

How LEAs went comprehensive will be considered fully in subsequent chapters; it suffices for the moment to note that the pattern of comprehensive reorganisation varies considerably from LEA to LEA – for, as is often remarked, the British educational system (especially in England) is run by a partnership between local and central government. By custom, convention, and law, local authorities have organised the schools in their area largely as they have thought fit. This large generalisation does require some qualification. Such organisation must be within the confines of education law (about which, however, there may be a variety of interpretations). And further, plans for radical changes to either individual schools, or to a local schools' system, do require the approval of the Secretary of State for Education. In the 1950s, the necessity for ministerial approval held back the early development of comprehensive schools; as in 1955 when a Conservative Minister of Education, David Eccles, 'declared that the government would "never agree to the assassination of the grammar school", as a prelude to announcing the policy of permitting the establishment of comprehensive schools only on new housing estates and in new towns, where there were no grammar schools in being' (Benn and Simon, 1970, p. 28).

Since the mid-1960s the boot has been for most of the time on the other foot – with central government urging and cajoling LEAs often reluctant to go comprehensive. And so they have – but very much along their own often idiosyncratic lines. Indeed, Caroline Benn and Brian Simon describe the approach to reorganisation in the late 1960s as 'bewilderingly various from area to area' (1970, p. 43). Indeed, after their exhaustive studies of LEA plans for going comprehensive at that time (the late 1960s), Benn and Simon comment: 'The impression given was that a few schemes were arrived at by default, rather than by serious investigation' (p. 44).

Given, then, the extent of local control, it is perhaps not surprising to find the reorganised secondary schools system 'bewilderingly various from area to area'. Following the 1944 Education Act most LEAs had two or at most three types of secondary schools. Children were selected for the grammar and technical schools at the age of eleven; the rest went to secondary moderns – perhaps too often the senior elementary schools with a change of name plate. The process was described as one of allocation, but few were taken in by this example of educational double-speak.

Most LEAs during reorganisation have retained the age of eleven as the appropriate age at which the child may start secondary schooling. Rather fewer LEAs have abandoned the attempt to sharply distinguish between primary and secondary education. These LEAs have created 'middle schools' which overlap the conventional primary and secondary sectors. (These schools are for administrative and statistical purposes 'deemed primary' or 'deemed secondary'.) Such LEAs have found it more expeditious, given the character of their schools, and the buildings that housed them, to abandon the division between primary and secondary at the age of eleven. In England in 1979 there were some 1374 middle schools. These schools housed children from eight, nine or ten to twelve, thirteen or fourteen years of age; and all permutations of these years. There were approximately 600 middle schools 'deemed secondary', many of them with fewer than 400 pupils. Thus these schools were on the small side for comprehensive schools, with all the limitations that implies for limitations in curriculum and teaching.

Such middle schools are complemented by upper schools, some of which take children aged from twelve to sixteen; some from twelve to eighteen; a large number from thirteen to eighteen; with a handful of schools diverging slightly from this pattern. These schools are larger than middle schools; many of them housing more than 1,000 pupils; and a few with getting on for 2,000. Those LEAs, operating a middle school system whose upper schools have no sixth form for pupils over the age of sixteen, have set up sixth-form colleges for this age group. (*Statistics of Education* indeed classifies such sixth-form colleges as comprehensive schools; although whether their admission arrangements are wholly without reference to ability and aptitude might be open to question in a number of cases.)

However, the majority of LEAs in England and Wales did not develop middle school schemes. In England in 1979, 1,470 comprehensive schools were for pupils between the ages of eleven and eighteen. Such schools are popularly known as 'all through' schools, and the pattern was the one that had the most approval from central government in the 1960s. This type of school ideally requires a school built to house it ('purpose-built'); and it is about the largest of the comprehensives. In 1979, 13 such schools had 2,000 pupils or more. (But many were created by bringing schools designed for quite other purposes into the 'split-site' comprehensive.) Somewhat similar are the 11–16 comprehensives. These, like some upper schools in middle school systems, require either sixth-form colleges or tertiary colleges to supplement them.

A number of LEAs did not have or could not procure the funds for purpose-built comprehensives. (As is so often the case, government was unwilling or unable to fund the reforms it was initiating politically, administratively, and legally.) Such LEAs created two-tier comprehensive schools – often by linking together a secondary modern school and a grammar school. The secondary modern (sometimes along with its staff) provided the nucleus for the junior school in such two-tier systems, whilst the grammar school was transformed into a two-tier senior school. Although in all these two-tier systems pupils begin at eleven, transfer to the senior school may take place at thirteen in one authority; fourteen in another. To make the confusion worse, in some LEAs transfer to a senior school is automatic; in others it may be optional, with pupils given the choice to remain at the lower or junior school until sixteen, the statutory leaving age, or to enter a 14–18 or 13–18 school. There is some debate about the virtues of optional schemes. Some supporters of comprehensive schools, as we shall see, believe that such schemes may be the means by which the grammar school is maintained (however disguised) and is, in addition, a device by which 'middle-class' parents in particular play the educational system to their advantage.

The above account is an attempt to shade in the outline of progress toward comprehensive reorganisation provided at the beginning of this introductory chapter. But it would be a mistake to believe that because secondary schools are now more or less reorganised on comprehensive lines we can look forward to a period of stability in these schools. Certainly the 1960s and 1970s were two decades of almost continuous change in many LEAs. It is difficult to estimate the consequences of this for the children passing through the schools at that time. Some of this change was brought about by an increase in population in the schools during the 1960s and 1970s. (The secondary school population reached its highest point in 1977/78 and is now declining ever more rapidly.) Nevertheless, some of the change was a consequence of secondary school organisation. Whatever the direct impact of school reorganisation on children, its effect on the staff of schools is very clear indeed. Reorganisation more often than not means the formal closure of schools, and their re-opening under a new headteacher and management at some later date. In some instances, teachers, with many years of experience in their own schools, have found themselves applying for the very job they have successfully filled for a decade or so. Headteachers have been, in a few instances, 're-appointed' as the deputy heads of schools where once they ruled the roost. In all cases salaries have been 'safeguarded': but this has not always been enough to repair the damage done to morale and professional pride.

Perhaps in many schools, undue complacency has been rightly questioned and disturbed. Such changes as described have provided, in addition, great opportunities – as always in times of great reform and turmoil – for the young, the able and the energetic. Young teachers have been able to make their mark. Some of the appointments to newly formed comprehensive schools were undoubtedly of this character, and at all levels of seniority. Nevertheless, there have been losses as well as gains. Intangible though such losses may be, it is difficult to believe they have not been made to the detriment of pupils and staff alike.

Radicals say in justification of revolutionary excess: 'You can't make omelettes without breaking eggs.' Schools have been abolished, or reshaped and reformed. Teachers have learnt, or have attempted to learn, new skills and approaches to teaching their subjects and pupils. There may have been more than one or two casualties along the way, as well as the destruction of schools with well established traditions and procedures. Has it all been worth it? In order to answer this question something must be said of the perceived strengths and weaknesses of the selective system that comprehensive schooling replaced. And that leads us back to the 1944 Education Act.

'Secondary education for all': the 1944 Act

In England and Wales, the 1944 Education Act created a legal framework for the educational system that has lasted to this day. The Act has been amended, and further Education Acts have extended the powers of local authorities and the schools. Acts of parliament not directly related to education have also had an impact on the organisation of schooling – notably the 1972 Local Government Act, which reformed local government, creating in the process new LEAs and abolishing old ones. The Safety at Work Act (1974) and the Sex Discrimination Act (1975) in their different ways have had some influence upon schools and their workings. But the broad pattern created by the 1944 Education Act still remains despite all these additions and amendments.

Historians of education argue that – at any rate in Britain – legislation about education is rarely innovatory. It is suggested that it largely consolidates the tendencies of the age. Certainly education was an area of government on which consensus was formerly sought. 'Rab' Butler, Minister of Education in Churchill's war-time and coalition administration, took great pains to consult all interested parties in education prior to presenting his bill (later to be approved as the 1944 Education Act) to parliament. The immediate post-war Labour government accepted the Act without murmur. Indeed there is every evidence that the Attlee administration regarded the Act as a well-laid stone in the foundations of the welfare (and socialist) state which they considered was the task of the post-war government to establish. The duty of the Ministry of Education was to administer the Act rather than to repeal or to amend it.

The 1944 Act is as interesting for what it failed to pronounce upon as what it did pronounce upon. For example, apart from the special case of religious instruction, it did not specify what was to be taught in schools, other than that it was the duty of LEAs to ensure that schools provide 'efficient instruction' (a phrase redolent of Victorian utilitarianism). In addition, although education was to be provided in three stages – primary, secondary and further – on how secondary education (our special concern here) was to be organised the Act is silent – except that 'the schools available for an area shall not be deemed to be sufficient unless they are sufficient in number, character and equipment to afford for all pupils as may be desirable in view of their differing ages, abilities and aptitudes' (Education Act, 1944, s. 8 (1)).

In the post-war years LEAs interpreted this section of the 1944 Act as giving legal support to the already existing diversity of secondary schools. Grammar, technical, and modern schools, it was believed, catered for the differing abilities and aptitudes of secondary school pupils. The eleven-plus test was the means by which children were to be selected for these different types of schools. Comprehensive school supporters were later to argue that this was a misinterpretation of the 1944 Act. Professor Pedley, for example, argued:

It might be thought that the obvious meaning [of section 8(1) of the Education Act, 1944] was that, just as a sufficient number of well-equipped primary schools was required to meet the very different needs of all the local children who went there, so each secondary school must have a full range of courses, staff, and equipment to meet the very different needs of these same children in due course whether they stayed at school beyond fifteen or not. (1978, p. 40.)

However, given the existence of grammar schools, themselves established by LEAs earlier in the century, and secondary moderns – both types of schools with rather different traditions and approaches – the policy of the LEAs in the immediate post-war years was not unreasonable. LEAs, in those years, were given advice by psychologists, such as Sir Cyril Burt (a pioneer educational psychologist with the London County Council) and educationalists such as Sir Cyril Norwood (former headmaster in turn of Bristol Grammar School, 1906, Marlborough College in 1916, and Harrow School in 1929), both that mental abilities could be measured scientifically and that 'rough groupings' could be made of: first, 'the pupil who is interested in learning for its own sake'; second, 'the pupil whose interests lie markedly in the field of applied science or applied art'; and third, of the pupil who 'deals more easily with concrete things than with ideas' (quoted in Maclure, 1973, pp. 201, 202).

Much innocent fun has been poked at both these Cyrils (and their notions) by the advocates of comprehensive schooling. Sir Cyril Burt's reputation as the high panjandrum of the science of educational psychology, already slipping towards the end of his long life, took a nose-dive after his death when a less than eulogistic biography (Hearnshaw, 1979) alleged that a number of his more celebrated psychological experiments had been faked. The Norwood Report, largely unread *in toto* as is the fate of most such reports, became a byword for a hypocritical defence of the educational *status quo*; as it was pointed out how rather too conveniently the Norwood typology justified the historically created tripartite division of schools into grammar, technical, and modern.

It is churlish to criticise the opponents of the eleven-plus for making the most of debating points so enticingly presented to them on a plate. Nevertheless, in essence, were the arguments employed by Burt and Norwood (and of those who thought similarly) altogether foolish? Burt believed that mental abilities could be objectively and scientifically measured. Perhaps he was naive in holding this view. But is it sensible to move from the premise that differences in mental abilities cannot be *accurately* measured to the conclusion that there are no such differences; or that they cannot be measured in however rough and ready a way (Norwood does speak only of 'rough groupings'); or that they cannot be made – however tentatively and provisionally – at the age of eleven?

Selection at eleven: unfair and unequal?

Grammar schools were usually well-respected except, of course, by those radicals who decried them for their 'middle-class' values, and who rarely stopped to consider whether such a critical stance is not one held exclusively by a section of middle-class intellectuals. Indeed comprehensive school advocates, at the beginning of their campaign, concentrated their fire on the iniquity and injustice of the eleven-plus selection tests, placing rather less emphasis on the positive virtues of comprehensive schools. Denis Marsden pointed out of Harold Wilson, for example, that 'as late as 1970 in a TV appearance he was still presenting the comprehensive school (in Gaitskell's earlier phrase) as a "grammar school for all"' (1971, p. 11).

Opinion on secondary moderns has been more neutral. Few defence committees sprang up declaring 'hands off our secondary modern'. But it may be wrong to assume that many parents and their children were necessarily dissatisfied with what such schools had to offer. However, secondary moderns did remain in the post-war years the poor relations of the grammar schools. Many factors helped to ensure this. Their buildings were often less than adequate. Many were originally built as Board schools in the 1870s and 1880s in the heart of big cities. In their time such schools had been a symbol of educational and social progress. (Many of them stand today a testimony to the enduring qualities of Victorian craftsmanship and materials. No doubt they will remain when many a post-war school built out of flimsy pre-fabricated materials has disintegrated.) But some of them, as the Newsom Report (1963) indicated, were slum schools in slums, with no playing fields, no libraries, no gymnasiums, and no rooms with equipment for practical activities.

In addition, in the distribution of resources, secondary moderns did rather less well than the grammar schools. In part this was because such schools had fewer and younger pupils than the grammar schools. The workings of a points-system by which schools were graded according to their size and the age of their pupils favoured the larger grammar schools with their bigger fifth and sixth forms. Thus grammar schools tended to be rather better equipped; to have more favourable teacher/pupil ratios; and to attract graduate teachers in greater numbers than secondary modern schools. Such differences made it difficult for LEAs and the DES to maintain the fiction of a 'parity of esteem' between the different types of school. Needless to say, opponents of the selective system made much of these differences.

From the point of view of parents, one obvious and striking difference between the two (or three) basic types of schools was that the grammar school held out at least the possibility of entry into white collar and professional employment, whilst the secondary modern seemed to destine its pupils for manual employment. Indeed, Professor Pedley, in *The Comprehensive School* (1978), draws a picture of the fashion by which the two or three basic types of schools mirror a tripartite division along social class lines in our society. The tripartite system could, therefore, be criticised on the grounds that it sustained social class divisions in society. Such divisions, it was claimed, were incompatible with a democratic and egalitarian society which was now a more universally accepted political and social idea. The research of the sociologists in the 1950s and 1960s filled out this picture in greater detail: providing masses of evidence that selection did broadly follow social class lines.[2] Children from the managerial and professional classes were proportionately considerably more likely to enter grammar schools and universities than children of parents in manual employment. The children of parents in unskilled manual employment were the least likely to take the royal road to the grammar school and university, and to the professional employment that lay at the end of that particular route.

The longitudinal surveys conducted by Dr J. W. B. Douglas and his team of indefatigable researchers revealed further inequalities. A decade or so later this pioneer research was replicated by the longitudinal survey initiated by the National Children's Bureau. Amongst further inequalities noted were the disparities in the provision of grammar schools and other selective schooling between LEAs. Some LEAs – notably in Wales – were well provided with grammar schools; others were not. There did not seem much of a rational pattern to this; rather, it depended upon historical accident, and the idiosyncratic decisions of education committees. Thus it was pointed out by the comprehensive school lobby that a child's chances of entry to a grammar school were to some extent dependent upon where he was living at the age of eleven. In addition, in the 1950s and 1960s, the child population was increasing rapidly, again making it seem as if grammar school entrance was a giant lottery, largely dependent upon such factors as geography and date of birth.

By the early 1960s, if not before, a battery of arguments had been mounted against the eleven-plus selection tests. It was argued that differences of ability between children could not be detected with accuracy. The notion of a fixed intelligence or mental ability that could be measured as one might a yard of cloth was no longer so firmly held. The abilities of children as measured in the eleven-plus test might reflect the coaching they received at home or in the school as much as their innate intelligence. Such a point of view appeared to be supported by the findings of the Crowther Report (1959), which, in looking at the measured intelligences of national servicemen, had come to the conclusion that a number of them may have been misplaced in their secondary schools.

Behind concern with the eleven-plus examination, however, there were increasing doubts about the selective (or tripartite) system. Did not the differences between grammar, technical and modern schools deny the promise held out in the 1944 Education Act of 'secondary education for all'? For, as Mary Warnock points out, whilst the tripartite system existed, the notion of the academic ladder remained 'but it became a concept which was not to be tolerated in public policy any more than the social ladder, an equally real, but equally deplorable idea; to be mentioned if at all only to be reviled' (1977, p. 41). Underpinning much of this argumentation is the notion of equality; and, in particular, the view that people must be treated equally, and without regard to wealth, or any contingent characteristics such as sex, race, or social class. In addition, it has come to be assumed, almost without question, that any form of inequality of treatment or distribution is in itself evidence of unjustice and unfairness. It is to a fuller scrutiny of these key notions that I turn in the next chapter.

2 The comprehensive ideal

'Some people, and I am one, want to use education as an instrument in pursuit of an egalitarian society.'
A. H. Halsey, Fellow of Nuffield College, Oxford, 1965.[3]

The eleven-plus attacked

The supporters of comprehensive reorganisation undermined the tripartite system by repeated attacks upon the eleven-plus system of selection. But this was not enough to promote the positive virtues of comprehensive schooling. If the methods employed by LEAs to select children for their schools were imperfect, it was not a sufficiently weighty argument in itself to show either that selection was wrong, or that grammar schools should be abolished. Indeed Michael Hinton, headmaster of a comprehensive school, Broadoak School, Weston-Super-Mare, argued in his *Comprehensive Schools: A Christian's View* that: 'This fact [the 11-plus is imperfect as a predictor of academic success] did not itself constitute a conclusive argument against segregation at eleven' (1979, p. 27). For such tests could be improved. It was often pointed out that eleven-plus selection had unfortunate consequences. Children who failed were humiliated by their failure; and those who were successful were perhaps over-rewarded for their success (or so it was said). Primary schools devoted too much time and effort to preparing their pupils for the tests. Zealous middle-class parents coached their children to help them to score highly on IQ tests, or employed teachers to do the job for them. If these practices were indeed as widespread as feared; or even if they were morally, socially and educationally as harmful as their detractors alleged, something could have been done to lessen their incidence and to mitigate any possible harm.

LEAs did alter their selection techniques and methods in response to criticism. The use of a one-day test to select pupils for grammar and technical schools was abandoned by LEAs; there was less reliance on IQ tests, and tests of ability at writing and sums. Instead, the reports and opinions of primary school teachers began to play a major part in selection.[4] Nevertheless, however hard LEAs tried to make their tests fair and objective, they could never satisfy their critics. For example, let us consider Tyrrell Burgess's comments on eleven-plus selection to be found in his book, *Inside Comprehensive Schools*; commissioned by the Department of Education and Science (DES) in 1970, presumably as part of an official attempt to explain and justify comprehensive reorganisation. Indeed Burgess, at that time an educational journalist, points out in the opening sentence of his Introduction: 'Schools are changing fast these days, and parents often feel bewildered by what goes on in them.'

Although Burgess accepted that 'the tests designed for the 11 plus are perhaps the best and fairest possible' (p. 4), this is not enough for him. One difficulty he draws attention to is a difficulty to be found in any system of examining. In many exams the measured abilities of a number of candidates may be so close that it is difficult to determine where to draw the pass/fail line. This is a genuine difficulty – but more can be made of it than it deserves. The danger is that of jumping from the premise, that in a number of cases it is truly difficult to decide whether a candidate be deemed to fail or pass, to the conclusion that there is no genuine difference of ability or capacity between those who can fulfil the requirements of the test or exam with ease, and those who palpably cannot.

In any selection test there are a number of candidates about whom it is a matter of arbitration whether they pass or fail. It cannot be other. In so far as such a selection test is a part of an education system, the possible harmful effects of such arbitration may be mitigated by permitting opportunities for re-sits – which many LEAs introduced. In addition, differences between grammar schools and secondary moderns in curricula and opportunities to sit external examinations began to diminish in the 1950s. Thus failure in the eleven-plus – for whatever reason – of children capable of the more academic and intellectually demanding work of the grammar school would not turn out to be such an unmitigated disaster. Indeed, from time to time, the academic success of an eleven-plus failure – perhaps in gaining a place in a university – would be trumpeted forth as indicating the failure of the selective system. It could be as plausibly used to illustrate the flexibility of the school system as a whole. For despite the oft-alleged rigidity of the selection system, there were many opportunities for the academically gifted young to find their level.

Burgess argues: 'It is clear that drawing a line between children of similar IQs and sending some to grammar schools and some to secondary moderns is absurd and unjust.' (p. 5). If drawing such a line is absurd and unjust it is so because there were separate schools for secondary school children, not because there were children of seemingly similar IQs through which lines must be drawn. But the iniquity, absurdity and injustice of selective schooling must be demonstrated independently of any such charges against the system of selection – which in any case Burgess has declared to be 'perhaps the best and fairest possible'.

Burgess, in his criticism of eleven-plus tests, touching on a matter of concern that will surface and re-surface in this book, claimed that although 'the tests seem to be educational, they are in effect social. The home backgrounds of children differ widely, and the children of manual workers or of poorly educated parents are likely to do less well in the normal intelligence test.' (p. 5).

Burgess, in making this point, was no doubt well aware of the research of the sociologists which in the 1950s and 1960s had so clearly revealed a strong and positive relationship between home and family background *and* success and failure at eleven-plus. Let us take such research findings for granted, and without posing any awkward questions of them, nevertheless ask what follows for eleven-plus selection if they are largely true. In what ways do the tests fail to be educational – that is, in testing educational attainments and potentialities in certain ways? We test a number of children to find out their abilities to read, write and to do their sums. Some are better than others. On further enquiry the former group tend to have parents who are deeply concerned about their children's educational progress, and who themselves value reading, writing, and numeracy. In addition – and perhaps, given their values this is not so surprising – such parents are, on the whole, clerks, teachers, managers, doctors, rather than miners, factory workers and dockers (although there are many exceptions). What conclusion do we draw from this enquiry? That the tests did not truly and genuinely test what they were intended to test, and to our certain knowledge truly did test? – that is, the abilities of the children to read, write and to do their sums. Surely not – the only adequate conclusion we may draw from our enquiry is that children from such backgrounds tend to do best in our selection tests and to show the greatest educational progress for their years. We cannot conclude that our tests have failed to test their abilities; and perhaps, in addition, their potential for further education.

Burgess also argues that even if we are able to measure and test the ability of children at eleven (and this is difficult to deny and Burgess never wholly denies it), 'to separate children into different kinds of schools would mean that we should have to be sure that their abilities did not change very much as they grew older' (p. 6). We expect the abilities of children to change as they grow older (providing perhaps, they are properly taught), therefore it follows we cannot separate them into different kinds of schools. But this conclusion is false as it depends upon the ambiguity of the premise. Burgess is conflating two notions. One is the widely accepted view that children's abilities change as they themselves grow and develop (with a little help from their teachers); and, the more contentious view is that the abilities of children relative to one another are constantly changing. No doubt Jill sometimes streaks ahead of Jack in her reading, and later Jack may close the gap – or open up other gaps with respect to other skills. Nevertheless, the view that the abilities of children relative to one another are inherently unstable is contentious, and may well have to be well supported independent of the virtues or otherwise of having separate schools.

In view of the many attacks upon eleven-plus selection by supporters of comprehensive schooling, it is worthwhile to consider a verdict upon this form of selection by the Labour Party politician, the late C. A. R. Crosland, Secretary of State for Education, 1965–67. It appears in his revisionist exposition of the socialist ideal, given a title that becomes more ironic as the years pass by: *The Future of Socialism*. In his chapter, 'The Influence of Education', he describes the eleven-plus test as being 'bitterly disliked and resented',[5] yet characterises the test in these terms:

> It was thought that a child's whole future was decided on a single day's test. No doubt much of the dislike was based on ignorance or exaggeration. The results in fact were never decided on a single day's test. Immense care was commonly taken over borderline cases. There was always provision (though often imperfect) for re-testing and transferring 'late developers'. And the better secondary modern schools began increasingly to provide advanced courses and thus a route to the higher occupation. (1956, p. 266)

It is difficult to believe that this passage was written by a politician hostile to the selective system, and who, as a Secretary of State for Education, initiated its destruction. Yet, for all his declared belief that 'much of the dislike [of eleven-plus selection] was based on fear and exaggeration', he could at the same time claim that 'there was quite sufficient truth in these intuitive fears to give them a genuine validity' (p. 267). Perhaps it was that as such fears were intuitively held they could not have other than 'a genuine validity', but it is difficult to pin down the 'sufficient truth' which he referred to. One cannot but suspect here that Crosland put on one side his own undoubted intelligence and knowledge of education in order to arrive at a conclusion more politically palatable to him.

It is difficult to know in considering the attacks and criticisms of the eleven-plus what precisely is the target. Are the methods of selection the object of attack? In which case critics should have been satisfied by the attempts to modify the examination: to make it fairer, and to mitigate its unintended consequences. The suspicion is that eleven-plus selection as such is unacceptable to the supporters of comprehensive schooling. If this is the case, is it selection at *eleven* that is to be condemned, whilst selection at sixteen or eighteen is to be considered as being perfectly all right: and, indeed, to be supported? The difficulty here is that most, if not all, of the arguments deployed against the eleven-plus may be used against selection at sixteen or eighteen – or selection within one school rather between two or three. The suspicion seems well grounded when one considers Michael Hinton's claim that: 'It is morally wrong to segregate children on the grounds of ability, especially when the division in fact reflects social rather than inherent differences.' (1979, p. 33)

The comprehensive principle

The attack upon the eleven-plus then, was a good deal more than a technical critique of a selection examination or the drawing of attention to disparities in the distribution of grammar schools throughout Britain. It was part of an attack upon selection – or segregation as it is more tendentiously called – and part and parcel of an outlook described as the comprehensive philosophy or principle. As Hinton remarks: 'It is not easy to define these principles clearly, nor to relate them to each other . . .' (1979, p. 55), nevertheless the attempt will be made here for the purpose of critical exegesis. And the reader will bear with me if '. . . the outcome of any attempt to do so would be a philosophy which would be far from commanding general assent' (Hinton, 1979, p. 53). Just so.

Whilst it is fair to say that comprehensive reorganisation was supported and sustained by reference to a theory of comprehensive schooling, it is equally true to remark that the tripartite system had its own theoretical underpinnings. Part of the task of the comprehensive school ideologists was indeed to undermine those intellectual foundations. It was to the disadvantage of the defenders of grammar schools (and the tripartite system) that these schools existed. Practice could be contrasted with theory and be found wanting. Supporters of comprehensive schooling were in the happier position of advocating the virtues of such schooling largely in the absence of the existence of such schools. Theories of how comprehensive schools ought to be working could not, then, be contrasted with an obdurate reality.

But what is the proper relationship between educational (and political) theories and humdrum practice and reality? Theory stands to practice in different ways. In one way, it informs practice: for example, if we believe (have a theory that) children with differing abilities ought to be taught both separately and differently, our practice may conform to that view. Alternatively, our theory may justify a practice adopted on entirely different grounds, thus theory may reflect and rationalise our practice rather than control it.

Practical theories, of which educational theories are a subset, are generally modified by practice. We change our views as to what is desirable to do, in the light of our increasing knowledge of what we can do. It is a criticism of the comprehensive school theorists that they seem unwilling to reconsider their theory in the light of what we now know of comprehensive school practice – as in the way that Professor Pedley (1978) argues that whilst there are many faults in our comprehensive school system, 'Its philosophy, however, remains unchanged.' (p. 8)

My view of the relationship between the educational theory and practice may be challenged. There are some who would argue that practical theories cannot be modified by practice – if the theory is correct, practice must be shaped to it come what may. In this alternative view of the relationship between theory and practice, human nature and human societies are seen as essentially plastic, to be moulded to whatever ideal pattern the theorist or planner thinks appropriate. I suggest that some comprehensive reformers tend to hold this view. It is, then, not surprising to find comprehensive reformers to be Marxist and socialists. This point is made most succinctly by John White, Lecturer in Philosophy at the London Institute of Education, who, in a house-magazine for the comprehensive school lobby, *Forum*, asserted that: 'Comprehensive schooling is an integral part of the socialist vision.' (1977, p. 60)

Indeed, John White's fear is that the malleability of the comprehensive school system may come to buttress an iniquitous and repressive capitalist order. This very possibility throws doubt, at least for John White, on the very worthwhileness of the comprehensive schools campaign itself for 'what conceivable point is there in pressing for a fully comprehensive system if that system can be remoulded to serve the needs of the economic order?'

(p. 60). Like many 'pressing for a fully comprehensive system', John White believes that such a reform must be paralleled by radical change in society as a whole. For as he in the same article plaintively asks: 'What point is there in demanding state-controlled curricula with socialist objectives if socialists are not always going to be in power?' 'Indeed', one is tempted to reply, although White himself argues that there is point – if only to assist in the evolution of society to its more desirable and desired socialist shape.

Later chapters will explore the relationship between comprehensive theory and practice, for yet another way lies open for a critical approach to the comprehensive philosophy. That is to attempt what Michael Hinton claims is not easy: 'to define these [comprehensive] principles clearly' and 'to relate them to each other' (p. 55).

Equality of opportunity

There is no doubt that the most fundamental notion underpinning the theory of comprehensive schooling is that of equality. However, supporters of comprehensive reorganisation do not belong to that group of naive egalitarians (if any there be) who believe that all human beings are, as a matter of undisputed fact, equal in all attributes. Comprehensive school egalitarians are not only willing to admit, but eager to point out, that children are indeed different in ability and aptitude: that is so long as such abilities and aptitudes may be largely attributed to the home and family background of children, to their social class and the neighbourhood in which they live. But egalitarians are often less willing to accept that human differences are biologically or genetically determined. Indeed, those psychologists, such as Professor H. J. Eysenck and Arthur Jenson, who make relatively modest claims for the place of genetic determination in the formation of human abilities are generally denounced by comprehensive reformers: first, on the quite reasonable grounds that such views are unfounded – reasonable, that is, given that counter-evidence is provided, and that there are grounds to believe the dismissal is based upon some form of scientific enquiry. Second, they are denounced because such views threaten strongly promoted opinions that most, if not all, differences between persons are determined by our upbringing and social environment. (And if we are so shaped, it follows that we may be reshaped to some more desired pattern – freer perhaps of old Adam.)

However for our purposes here, it is sufficient to note with

Professor Pedley that 'No two children are the same; that is a truism.' (1978, p. 29). Advocates of comprehensive schooling are more likely to believe that – without question – equality is a good thing and the more of it the better. Thus they belong to that group of egalitarians so entertainingly brought to our notice by the philosopher, David Cooper, in his book, *Illusions of Equality* (1980). Cooper quotes A. H. Halsey, Professor of Social and Administrative Studies, University of Oxford, and Adviser (1965–68) to the Secretary of State for Education under a Labour government, as saying 'the role of education must largely be to maintain such a society [a society of equals] once it has been attained' (Cooper, 1980, p. 1). And Cooper further quotes Professor Brian Simon as claiming that education's 'objective should be equality' (p. 1). Such egalitarians are forever asserting the virtues of a more equal society, rarely pausing to detail in what specific features such a society shall be equal, or what are the justifications for such equality. It is enough that equality prevails.

On rather more common ground with their opponents, the comprehensive school lobby have claimed that comprehensive reorganisation is the means by which we shall increase equality of opportunity for children. For Professor Pedley the comprehensive school is 'justified principally by the accepted need to give maximum opportunity for self-fulfilment to each and all . . .' (1978, p. 99). And head master Michael Hinton condemns selection at eleven because it reduces rather than increases opportunities; 'Segregation was, then, seen to be wrong not just because a minority of children were clearly misplaced but because the vast majority – and society as a whole – could benefit from a wider provision of courses than a school in a tripartite system could provide.' (1979, p. 30). Both these statements suggest that comprehensive schooling is about opportunity to be offered fairly and equally to all.

The advantage of the principle of equality of opportunity to the comprehensive school lobby is that it is a principle to which most people in the second half of the twentieth century assent. The disadvantage of employing such a principle, however, was that it had been used to justify selective schooling. Indeed R. H. Tawney, a scholar and committee man of much influence on the Labour Party's educational policies, had employed the principle in that way in *Secondary Education for All* (1922): a seminal work as far as educational policy in Britain is concerned. Tawney argued that: 'all normal children, irrespective of the income, class, or occupation of their parents, may be transferred at the age of eleven and from the primary or preparatory school to *one type or another of secondary school* and remain in the latter till sixteen' (p. 7, my italics). For Tawney, equality of opportunity was achieved by education provided for children irrespective 'of the income, class, or occupation of their parents'; but not necessarily by providing children with identical opportunities within one school. Indeed in 1922 he argued that 'within the secondary system of each [local authority] there must be more than one school' (p. 14).

If the principle of equality of opportunity may be used to justify *both* selective and non-selective schooling perhaps it is too vague and ambiguous to be much help for policy-making. What, indeed, is meant by the principle; and what follows for practice from it? Typically, as is often remarked, the principle is evoked to justify the removal of specific barriers to scarce opportunities. Tawney, for example, stated in *Equality*: 'The idea that differences of educational opportunity among children should depend upon differences of wealth among parents is a barbarity.' (1952 edition, p. 157.) Make the schooling of children independent of the wealth of their parents, and a specific obstacle to equality of opportunity is removed. It is perhaps for that reason the Universal Declaration of Human Rights states: 'Education shall be free, at least in the elementary and fundamental stages.' (Article 26(1)). The wealth of parents, and their social status, has come to be seen as irrelevant to the education of their children, and should not be a barrier to their opportunities. In an historical perspective this was not self-evident: many influential Victorians believed that the education children receive ought to be consistent with the social standing of their parents. For such Victorians it seemed clear and indisputable that educating (say) the son of an artisan above his station in life did little good for him, and less for a well-ordered society (perhaps by encouraging discontent and sedition). In contrast, 'equality of opportunity' as an educational and political slogan has been so persuasive because it appears to offer the prospect of a more efficient society (the most capable chosen for the more demanding jobs in society), and a more fulfilled life for individuals as we all find, more or less, the social, occupational, and intellectual level suited to our capacities.

Antony Flew has argued that 'what has usually been meant by "equality of opportunity" would be better described as open competition for scarce opportunities' (1981, p. 45). It is the element of competition, that seems a part of the notion of equality of opportunity, that lessens its popularity as a principle with the more egalitarian minded supporter of comprehensive schooling. Again, the notion of opportunities, which may or may not be taken, or may be taken by individuals or groups to different lengths, is deeply worrying to some egalitarians. Tawney says (somewhat ironically) that: 'Rightly interpreted, equality meant, not the absence of violent contrast of income and condition, but equal opportunities of becoming unequal.' (1952, p. 105). However, if in Brian Simon's words education's 'objective should be equality', the principle of equality of opportunity may have to be abandoned (or re-interpreted or re-stated in some more acceptable form) if it provides only 'equal opportunities of becoming unequal'.

Torsten Husén, Professor of Education, University of Stockholm, and as Director of the Institute for International Education a promoter of universal comprehensive schooling, in a recent book, *The School in Question* (1979), sees it as a *dilemma* of schooling that by creating 'competencies' (Husén's expression) a school system 'almost by necessity creates differences. . . . The school cannot at the same time serve as an equaliser and as an instrument that establishes, reinforces, and legitimises distinctions' (p. 89). The choice is then quite stark for the committed egalitarian: between a school that makes children more equal, and one that through its teaching inevitably widens the gap between the least and the most capable child. An egalitarian, it may be presumed, must choose equality – but at the cost of abandoning the principle of equality of opportunity.

Husen quotes the opinion of James R. Gass 'that policies that derive from the notion of making access opportunities formally equal have proven to have a "disappointingly limited impact". The reappraisal inspired by the partial failure of previous policies would have to consider measures that go beyond the removal of entrance "obstacles to positive political measures of compensations and support, with the ultimate aim of a more equal social outcome"' (Husén, 1979, p. 76). (James R. Gass is, like Husén, a research mandarin, and the Director of the Centre for Educational Research and Innovation (CERI).) Equality of educational opportunity, as understood by an earlier generation of educational reformers has been a 'partial failure' it seems. It has failed because schools have not become equalisers, and because those children that take up opportunities on offer remain obdurately similar in social background to those children who were successful at school in earlier decades. Equality of opportunity ('making access opportunities formally equal') has failed if judged in terms of 'the ultimate aim of a more equal social outcome'.

For those, of course, who are not committed to such an ultimate aim, the principle of equality of opportunity (perhaps in Flew's redescription: 'open competition for scarce opportunities') still has some virtue for educational policy; although we may agree with Tawney that 'like other respectable principles, it is encouraged to reign, provided it does not attempt to rule' (1952, p. 106). However, our doubts about the principle may not be quite those that Tawney had in mind. Tawney's reservations were: first, that the principle was likely to promote inequality of outcome; and, second (anticipating later objections) it was lamentably difficult to remove *all* obstacles to open competition for scarce opportunities. What he had in mind were those differences in capacity which had their origin in family life (to which others might add genetic factors). No doubt Tawney underestimated the degree to which the state might be encouraged to control the total social environment: as in the already noted suggestion by the Director of the CERI, James R. Gass, that what requires consideration are 'positive political measures of compensations and support, with the ultimate aim of a more equal social outcome'. Here we might reflect upon the view of Professor Hayek that to achieve a literally interpreted equality of opportunity 'government would have to control the whole physical and human environment for all persons, and have to endeavour to provide at least equivalent chances for each; and the more government succeeded in these endeavours, the stronger would become the legitimate demand that, on the same principle, any still remaining handicaps must be removed – or compensated for by putting extra burden on the still relatively favoured' (Hayek, 1976, p. 85).

It is difficult, then, in the light of the above, to see how the principle of equality of opportunity may be used exclusively to justify comprehensive schooling. For, as noted, it may just as plausibly be employed to support a system of selective schooling: as in the way that many LEAs interpreted, in the immediate postwar years, the injunction of the 1944 Education Act that education is to be provided 'to afford for all pupils such variety of instruction and training as may be desirable in view of their different ages, abilities and aptitudes' (s. 8(1)). Indeed, it may well be that comprehensive schooling fails to provide opportunities for children who otherwise would have bloomed in the selective grammar schools now abolished.

Consider, for example, Michael Hinton's response to the argument that able children 'have a right to better schooling than average children, partly because their talents are of more value to society' (1979, p. 56). For Hinton, this argument is weak 'morally and socially'. He claims that 'the "ability" of able children is usually the effect of a favoured background' (p. 56). (Note here the use of sneer quotes around 'ability' – perhaps to indicate this is not true or genuine ability; or, perhaps, more subtly that differences of ability between children are in the minds of their teachers rather than to be discerned in some more objective sense.) It is puzzling to know what is being objected to more strongly: that one child might be more able than another, or that ability might be traced to 'a favoured background'. It is difficult to see however, from the teacher's point of view, what is the relevance of the origin or source of ability; we may be thankful for talent however formed. The relevance of the favoured background is revealed when we read further that the resources of the community should not 'be used to reinforce advantage' (p. 56). Why we should not help to develop ability already clearly demonstrated is not made clear. We can only infer that this would strengthen inequalities already present in the school. Hinton clearly believes that the school must equalise rather than develop 'competencies'.

Hinton also argues that the able child does not make better use of his education; rather, 'He gets further more quickly with the same amount of teaching' (p. 56). And yet this might be a criterion for deciding who makes the most of the teaching he receives. If the objective of Hinton is equality of outcome rather than equality of opportunity, we might conclude that the able child ought to be taught less fully, competently, or carefully than his less able contemporaries.

If we turn from these abstractions to consideration of a specific example, albeit fictitious or hypothetical, the restraints on equality of opportunity implicit in Hinton's outlook may show even more clearly. Let us suppose that we find amongst our pupils a child of outstanding scientific bent. Let us freely imagine that such a child is interested in the biological and physiological sciences; and, in addition, shows neatness and deftness in handling of materials and practical experiments. Here we might have the ideal candidate for a career in medicine – indeed a future highly skilled surgeon. It is difficult to deny that such a child may have a talent and ability – in that cant phrase – of value to society. Indeed, self-interest may promote the thought that at some stage in our lives, or of those of our nearest and dearest, we may require the attentions of such a skilled medical practitioner. In addition, a wider compassion may lead us to consider the value of developing such skills for the good of all: a sentiment particularly dear to the more collectivist minded in the comprehensive school lobby.

Is there, then, not a very strong case for developing such a talent; for, indeed, devoting rather more teaching and time to such a child than to his or her less able companions? Equality of opportunity may have initially led us to have offered equivalent opportunities to all; but given that we have here one child capable of making the most of those opportunities, both in his or her own interest and in that of community, there is nothing in the principle demanding that we fail to provide those opportunities for that child which are wholly consistent with his or her abilities. And if further we discover the child comes from a 'favoured background' – is, perhaps, the son or daughter of medical practitioners – should we waver in our conviction that we ought to do our best to foster this talent, even if this means providing a better education for him or her than for less able contemporaries?

The principle of equal value

P. E. Daunt, formerly headmaster of Thomas Bennett compre- hensive school (and later to become a member of the Education Directorate of the Commission of the European Community where 'much of his work is concerned with the achievement of educational equality') enunciates 'the principle of equal value' as the preferred alternative to that of equality of opportunity in his *Comprehensive Values*. Daunt contrasts two views of com- prehensive schooling. One he calls 'meritocratic' (following Denis Marsden, 1969). A comprehensive school system seen from this point of view is simply better and more efficient than a selective system. Comprehensive schools are 'not intended to be performing any essentially different central functions from the selective system but performing the same functions more flexibly and therefore both more fairly and more efficiently' (Daunt, 1975, p. 12). Underpinning both systems is the principle of equality of opportunity. But for Daunt such a principle is inadequate as a principle of equality. For example, it would permit a comprehen- sive school to organise on selective lines, therefore defeating the object of the exercise. Such a point is recognised by Professor Pedley who in defining a comprehensive school ('The compre- hensive secondary school is simply an extension of the compre- hensive primary school, and has the same aims' (1978, p. 25)) nevertheless cautions: 'Such a school will not however be divided into distinct, separately organised sides, such as grammar, technical and "modern"' (p. 26).

Daunt argues that 'there is one essential principle of compre- hensive education which can be clearly identified (p. 15). . . . It is a principle of equal value' (p. 16). Indeed Daunt is so impressed with this stated principle that he describes it as the comprehen- sive principle ('I believe that there is such an idea, which I shall call *the comprehensive principle*, and that it can be clearly identified and expressed.' (p. 10)). Daunt rather more fully identifies and expresses 'the guiding principle' as being that '*the education of all children is held to be intrinsically of equal value*'. (p. 16.) The importance of this principle for Daunt is made clear by his remark that the principle 'commands not merely assent but allegiance . . .' (p. 17).

Such an important principle demands attention prior to assent – never mind allegiance. Though most clearly stated by Daunt, the principle (or something like it) is echoed in Professor Pedley's 'concept of equal worth; that is, all equally deserving and needing such aids to personal growth as we can give' (1978, p. 29). Michael Hinton declares his support for Daunt's principle for which he provides a gloss: 'To put it crudely, everyone matters as much as everyone else, and our school system should reflect the fact' (1979, p. 53).

The principle is high sounding and appropriate for speech days – except that such treats are forbidden in the more progressive comprehensive school – but does it mean anything? Daunt is well aware of this objection as he concedes: 'It is fair to ask what does the principle imply more than a hazy sentiment of general benevolence? How does the principle come to grips with real priorities for action and the distribution of resources?' (p. 22). In what sense can it be as Daunt claims it must be: 'the guiding principle' to comprehensive school practice? The principle of equal value cannot be taken literally because resources are limited. It is also unrealistic to believe pupils and their parents capable of interpreting the idea literally; they naturally have a vested interest. No doubt the principle, it may be said, is a principle of rational action for school teachers; not parents and pupils. Nevertheless, Daunt defends his principle by arguing that the school has much to learn from the family; the family, he says, ought to be the model for the school. Is he right?

Daunt realises that many families do not match up to the ideal family. Parents may indeed value one child rather more highly than others: there are 'favourite sons' and 'black sheep'. Nevertheless Daunt argues that the ideal family is one that most flesh and blood families attempt to copy; and by whose standards all families are judged. Even granted all this: ought and can schools copy the family? Families serve many purposes; schools a much more limited range. Membership of a family is life-long; that of a school very much less. The relationships created within a school – particularly the day school attended by most children – are similarly limited and transitory. Teachers may stand *in loco parentis*; but they are not the parents of the children they teach; and they are not tied to their pupils by those bonds of familial affection to be found between members of families. It would be unfair and manipulative to demand of adults and children the loyalty and love to be found in the best families, for the formal institutions of society such as schools. Daunt's argument then fails with this analogy. The family is only a partial and limited model for schools; and a model whose limitations require to be widely recognised.

At best the principle of equal value is either a statement of formal equality of consideration, or a plea for equality of respect. If the former, stripped of its more sentimental aspects, it is a way of stating that every pupil counts as one; and as such demands an equality of consideration, if not of treatment, with any other pupil. Expressed in this way the principle is not inconsistent with inequalities of treatment and teaching; and with the notion of competition for scarce opportunities. For instance, given that the resources for teaching electrical engineering are limited, all candidates for access to such scarce opportunities are given equality of consideration. This does not imply that all are to be chosen to follow the course, and to be afforded access to such scarce opportunities. Seen in this light the principle of equal value is wholly congruent with the principle of equality of opportunity (at least in terms of Flew's redescription of the principle as 'competition for scarce opportunities').

Nevertheless, one might suspect that the principle of equal value may be equivocally interpreted as demanding equal treatment rather than equal consideration. Pedley tells us that 'The average Englishman is confused about the meaning and implications of equality.' (1978, p. 27.) Apparently, this average Englishman is so confused about equality that 'He takes it for granted that equality implies flat uniformity, that equality in education would impose the same subjects, the same teaching methods, the same pace of progress, on pupils, who obviously differ enormously in their ability interests and characters.' (1978, p. 27.)

'Equality' has become an hurrah word. As we have seen, to describe something as equal is nowadays to praise it. For example an equal society is, without question, to be preferred to an unequal one, irrespective of what might be equal, and without attempting to justify such equalities. Indeed, it is widely believed, without question, that inequalities require justification, whilst equality is self-evidently justifiable. Given this climate of opinion, any self-respecting propagandist will want to gather to his pet cause that approbation which hurrah words encourage. Nevertheless, 'flat uniformity' does not sound so good – nor is it in any way defendable from what we know of the varying abilities and attributes of children: a truth about children never very seriously denied by the comprehensive school lobby ('No two children are the same; that is a truism.') So the much desired equality may mean, at one and the same time, equality in the everyday and commonplace sense of this much abused word, and 'the full development of everyone's talents' (Pedley 1978, p. 27) along lines infinitely diverse and unequal: as what is diverse cannot be equal. For in Pedley's words, which would not discredit that most enthusiastic Black Paper supporter, Rhodes Boyson: 'We need a frank recognition that individuals are unique, their differences immensely (indeed immeasurably) varied and demanding great flexibility of both teachers and administrators.' (p. 34.) That equality of consideration is by no means equality of treatment or equality of access is made quite clear by Tawney, who in *Equality* argues: 'The more anxiously, indeed, a society endeavours to secure equality of consideration for all its members, the greater will be the differentiation of treatment which, when once their common human needs have been met, it accords to the special needs of different groups and individuals among them.' (1952, p. 39.) A sentiment echoed by Michael Hinton who states: 'People are different and, once their common humanity has been recognized, they should be treated differently.' (1979, p. 57.)

But if pupils 'once their common humanity has been recognised', are treated differently, and taught in sets, streams, and classes appropriate to such differences, what then of the comprehensive school in which selection plays no part? The principle of equal value (if this is not a principle of equality of treatment; of uniformity) leads us once again to differences of teaching and curriculum appropriate to the differences between pupils in ability and aptitude. And yet such differentiation is as condemned within the comprehensive school as it was between schools in the tripartite system. But there is nothing to rule out such differentiation in the treatment of pupils – once it is denied that principle is one of uniformity and equal treatment.

Perhaps what is of fundamental concern is equality of respect rather than consideration, access, or outcome. Pedley, Daunt, *et al*, are pleading that we, the community, respect children equally whatever their capacity, or courses of study followed. Richard Peters, Professor of the Philosophy of Education at the London Institute of Education, puts this well when in his *Ethics and Education* he argues: 'It is possible for a system to be fair, in that differences in treatment are grounded on relevant differences between people, and yet be permeated by attitudes of contempt and deference which seem thoroughly objectionable.' (1970,

p. 14.) As Peters points out 'better at' rapidly becomes misleading when abbreviated to 'better'. It is the contempt on the one hand, and the deference on the other, that is accorded to one set of pupils and students as opposed to another, that rightly disturbs the comprehensive school supporters. That is why the term 'segregation' is so often used where defenders of the tripartite schemes preferred selection or (rather misleadingly) allocation. Pedley speaks of the 'forced segregation of children in separate schools, with the awful implications of daily, publicly, hammering home a child's officially assessed inferiority . . .' (1978, p. 46).

But Pedley misrepresents the cause of the humiliation that may follow from failure to achieve the coveted scholarship place. The cause here lies in a wider contempt for those who are not capable of reaching certain intellectual standards. It is we who are only too ready to scorn the village idiot, and to admire the sharp-witted rascal. It is not selection in itself that is at fault but our view of its consequences. Creating comprehensive schools will not, therefore, minimise both our feelings of hurt if on the receiving end, or our readiness to denigrate and dismiss if on the giving end. The disgrace and shame of failing the eleven-plus (if such there was) is eliminated by abolishing the selective system that, if not the cause of such feelings, inadvertently became, as Professor Peters remarks, its channel. However, not a great deal is gained if, within the comprehensive school, the whole process starts again. A school may teach its pupils differently based upon relevant differences between them. Some pupils become more highly esteemed than others, both within and without the school. The remedial group becomes known as the 'daft class'; whilst those working for 'A' levels and preparing for universities are seen in a very different light. Schools may underline, or attempt to underplay, the effects of selecting pupils for its variety of courses. It is difficult to see, if people insist on valuing different activities differently, how much schools can do about it. Or to expect it to be less endemic in comprehensive schooling than it was in the selective system. Indeed, as we will see, differences *between* comprehensive schools (as well as within them) have appeared.

Nor is it necessarily true that children were all shamed by failing the eleven-plus, or all that raised up by success. Indeed, Professor Pedley, in a brief autobiographical note, tells us that when translated from his village elementary school to ancient grammar school: 'I felt a guilty turncoat when the elementary school children of the town chanted "Grammar, grammar match-stalks" derisively at us as we walked long-trousered through the cobbled streets.' (p. 35.) In the tripartite system, up to a quarter of children at eleven-plus were selected for grammar and technical schools. These proportions were such as to ensure (although this was never intended) that the selected children could never conceive of themselves as an elite, to be bound together so as to form some future ruling order. And those rejected as unsuitable for selective schools were indeed the majority – and no doubt gained the comfort that comes from being a part of the larger portion. Indeed, Pedley's autobiographical notes – and some observations to be found in Brian Jackson and Denis Marsden's *Education and the Working Class* (1962) may lead us to the tentative conclusion that it can be the *selected* pupil (particularly from the working class) who can be made to feel humiliation and hurt.

Social unity and comprehensive schooling

So far it has been largely assumed that the supporters of comprehensive reorganisation were concerned with educational benefits. Comprehensive schools, it has been noted, were justified by Pedley 'principally by the accepted need to give maximum opportunity for self-fulfilment to each and all . . .' (1978, p. 99). Nevertheless, it is important to recall, as John White puts it, that comprehensive schooling 'is an integral part of the socialist vision' (1977, p. 60). For a socialist this vision is of a future society – a heaven on this earth rather than one beyond the blue horizon. The precise characteristics of this future society are difficult to itemise, but it is generally suggested that such a society would be free of those conflicts that so bedevil the societies of the present. Such a society would be free of conflicts that have their origin in the *divisions* of society: for example, those of class, race, religion, age, and gender, to name some of the more fundamental. Such a society, we may be told, will be without hierarchies based upon whatever – age, income, skill, occupation. Co-operation and equality, rather than competition for scarce opportunities and resources, will be the order of the day. Indeed, the question as to how such scarce resources are to be distributed, which has vexed mankind for generations, will be resolved by following the Marxist principle: 'To each according to their needs, from each according to their abilities.'

What part can comprehensive schools play in bringing the socialist vision to fulfilment? As Hinton puts it, 'We ought to be one society and our education system should play its part in creating that unity.' (1979, p. 33.) It can be done principally in two ways: first by creating comprehensive schools themselves – for such schools are 'an integral part' of a future socialist society. If there can be a society without divisions of any sort – one society –

then selective schooling may be considered otiose. Second, comprehensive schools can prepare their pupils to be members of a future socialist society – even if it has not yet come into being.

A lot then depends upon our view of the socialist vision. If we do not share this vision then the argument clearly falls. It is certainly doubtful whether many people in Britain are socialists now (whatever may have been the case in the reign of good King George). Electoral support for the Labour Party has waned for many years. It is also doubtful, despite the constitution of the Labour Party, that what electoral support it now enjoys is based upon support for socialism, and a wish to bring to fulfilment the socialist vision. In so far as comprehensive schooling is an integral part of such a vision, it cannot by that token claim much support and legitimacy.

For why, indeed, ought we to be 'one society'? British society is plural rather than singular and monolithic. It is made up of many diverse groupings loosely based upon different affinities: religion; race; age; sex; shared interests, etc. No doubt a plural society faces many problems in accommodating and reconciling these groupings. There must, in addition, be some degree of tolerance, and agreement on ground rules, for the society to hang together at all. But it remains difficult to see why we must be *one* society: singular in outlook and purpose; uniform rather than diverse. Again, the stress that, quite rightly, supporters of comprehensive reorganisation themselves put on diversity and individuality seems to belie this stated belief that social unity is an overriding goal which schools must play their part in achieving.

Parents and pupils who do not share the socialist vision, nor wish to live in one society, may find some consolation and support in a verdict of the United States of America's Supreme Court in 1925. The judges were adjudicating on a bill in Oregon which insisted 'that the public school should mix children of all the people – all ethnic groups, all economic classes – in order to promote social solidarity'. The Supreme Court's reply was that the law was unconstitutional, and an 'unreasonable interference with the liberty of parents to direct their children's education' (quoted in Ravitch, 1978, p. 61). At a rather more homely level we may take comfort from some remarks made by the late C. P. Snow, the novelist, who when, as Lord Snow and serving as Parliamentary Secretary to the Minister of Technology in the Labour government, he explained to the House of Lords why his son was at Eton: 'It seems to me that if you are living in a fairly prosperous home it is a mistake to educate your children differently from most of the people they know socially.' (quoted in Boyd, 1973, p. 141.)

In addition, it is not sensible to prepare children for a society not yet in being (putting on one side the virtues of that future order). Our society remains – to the despair no doubt of good socialists – incorrigibly competitive and hierarchical. Whatever its faults, that is the society we have to prepare children for. We may not wish our children to accept such a society uncritically, nor would we want to stop them as mature adults from attempting to reform and reshape it. Nevertheless, only foolhardy parents make no attempt to prepare their children for society as it is, rather than how they might wish it to be. Of course, what is being advocated here is not some amoral adaption to a social order, however abhorrent. I take it that British society, for all its faults, is not totally without its virtues. All I am suggesting is that schools may quite legitimately see it as their task to prepare their pupils for our society as it is, rather than for some socialist utopia of universal co-operation and equality. Nor does it seem reasonable (or fair) to demand that schools play any part in bringing this order into being. Create the socialist society first, and then devise whatever schools are required for this new society. It may immediately be remarked that comprehensive schools must, *ipso facto*, be a part of such an order. That may well be so (although in speculating about future society, who knows?); but that does not, in itself, prop up the argument. If the argument in support of comprehensive schools is that it is an intrinsic part of the socialist vision, then if we do not share the vision, we must reject this argument for comprehensive schools. (Of course, we may be convinced on other more educational grounds of the value of comprehensive schooling.)

Although this is perhaps unimportant to those that have no wish to fulfil the socialist vision, it may be worth noting that there is, anyway, precious little evidence that schools would be effective towards that end. Professor Husén quotes the well-known educationalists and sociologists, Charles Frankel and A. H. Halsey, as saying that, 'Too much has been claimed for the power of educational systems as instruments for wholesale reform of societies which are characteristically hierarchical in their distribution of chances in life as between races, classes, the sexes and as between metropolitan/suburban and provincial/rural population.' (1979, p. 76.)

The above completes my attempt to define the principles underpinning the comprehensive school ideology. In part, I have argued, it is defended by reference to the principle of equal opportunity. Supporters of comprehensive schooling claim that selective systems of education reduce opportunities whilst comprehensive schooling increases them. The truth of this may have to be discovered in practice. However, comprehensive school advocates readily admit that children differ in ability and aptitude. Lady Simon of Wythenshawe, an early advocate of comprehensive schooling, concedes in her *Three Schools or One* (1948) that 'There is, of course, a considerable amount of truth in the recognition not only of different abilities in children but of differing amounts of those abilities in each child.' (in Silver (ed.), 1973, p. 109.) Given these differing abilities, comprehensive school supporters also admit that children cannot be treated equally – 'flat uniformity', as Pedley put it, is to be abhorred. Selection goes out *between* schools, only, it seems, by the logic of the argument advanced by comprehensive school supporters themselves, to return *within* the schools. (So long that is – in the contradictory fashion of comprehensive school advocates – as the children are not categorised, or streamed, set or banded.)

It is well recognised by the supporters of comprehensive schools, that as a principle 'equality of opportunity' may be two-edged. It may be used to justify selection between schools and within them: as all that may be equal is competition to make the most of what opportunities are available. In addition, as Tawney observed, equality of opportunity does not guarantee equality of outcome; rather the reverse as it may more clearly amount to the opportunity to be unequal.

Sensitive to these difficulties, more radical advocates of comprehensive schooling (such as P. E. Daunt) replaced, or supplemented, the notion of equality of opportunity (despite its obvious attraction as an instrument of persuasion) for the principle of equal value. This, I have argued, when not high-sounding cant, is either a (formal) principle of equal consideration, or a plea for equality of respect. As the former, it offers no specific defence of comprehensive schooling as opposed to a more selective system. As the latter, it is doubtful that the root cause of any lack of respect for those unsuccessful in terms of formal schooling is to be found in a selective system as such. Rather, the cause is greatly deeper; and is more a matter of general attitudes to those that fail to match up certain standards of intellectual competence. (This point, although not without some truth in so far as people are humiliated by failure at school, and by those that scorn such failure, nevertheless, may be exaggerated: as many children and adults have no great regard for either success at school, or intellectual achievement in general.)

Finally, I have argued that as comprehensive schooling has been described as 'an integral part of the socialist vision' it can well be rejected by those not sharing such an outlook. For if it is indeed a socialist society we truly want, let us establish it first;

rather than reshaping our schools to reshape our society: a reform which in any case may be quite fruitless. So far I have considered the theory or ideology of comprehensive schools not their practice. The theory, or principles, discussed up to now were used – in so far as they permitted – in guidance for policy-makers. How comprehensive schools came into being in Britain, and to what degree the general policy exemplified comprehensive school ideology, will be discussed in the following chapters.

3 The rise of comprehensive schooling

'The grammar school will be abolished over my dead body.'
Harold Wilson, Labour Prime Minister, 1964.[6]

Comprehensive reorganisation: popular movement or unpopular conspiracy?

How did the comprehensive principle, outlined and discussed in the previous chapter, become public policy? One difficulty in answering this question is that the books to which one might look for an answer, take it for granted that comprehensive education is a good thing. Perhaps it is impossible to write any historical account without some bias in one direction or another. Total impartiality may be impossible in historical enquiry. And, however attractive as an ideal objective historical scholarship might be, it may as an ideal be very difficult to approach when the subject is recent events; and events that stir up controversy and create emotion.

Nevertheless, the degree of bias in support of comprehensive reorganisation in books on the development of secondary education is startlingly strong. This is 'whig' history with a vengeance. Typically, the move towards comprehensive schooling is seen as a progress towards greater equality; and, therefore, by definition more just and good. This progress is described as inevitable and inexorable. In *The Evolution of the Comprehensive School, 1926–1972*, written, as noted before, with a readership of student teachers particularly in view, David Rubinstein and Brian Simon claimed that: 'the movement towards comprehensive education is bigger than particular political parties and . . . has taken shape without the support of any of the major parties. Fundamentally this movement is a reflection of deep-seated economic and social changes. It seems unlikely that it can now be reversed . . .' (1973, p. 119).

Rubinstein and Simon were not alone in seeing comprehensive reorganisation as being the product of deep-seated economic and social forces. For example, Elizabeth Halsall, a lecturer in the Department of Educational Studies, University of Hull, in *The Comprehensive School, Guidelines for the Reorganization of Secondary Education*, similarly claimed that: 'in education, as in other aspects of political and social life, there are general movements which affect large areas of the world and which it is pointless to oppose, since they are powered by deep motivations of great force.' In education, it seems, these general movements were pointing in the direction of the reorganisation of secondary schools on comprehensive lines. Halsall adds (threateningly?): 'Opposition to such deep and powerful forces is futile.' (1973, p. 1.)

Such pronouncements may serve two purposes. One is to put heart into those leading and supporting the demand for secondary school reorganisation. No doubt many people relish the notion of taking part in a mass movement towards some desirable goal, particularly if it is postulated that they are pulled along in the agreed direction by mysterious social forces (perhaps somewhat akin to magnetism). No doubt also, this may create a 'bandwagon effect', by which people, indifferent to, sceptical of, or cynical about the desirability of the destination, will nevertheless clamber aboard for fear of being left behind. The second effect is that such a line of argument may demoralise the opposition. For what are they opposing but, in the words of Rubinstein and Simon, 'deep-seated economic and social changes' or according to Halsall: 'general movements . . . powered by deep motivations of great force' to which opposition is futile. The campaign is won almost before it has begun.

However, if we begin to look at how comprehensive reorganisation actually took place, a rather different picture begins to emerge. It is not mysterious and occult social forces, or general movements (however powered), that transformed secondary schooling. On the contrary, case-studies of local authority policy-making, along with accounts of the inner workings of political parties, demonstrate that it is men who make history: and very often a small number of them at that. Nevertheless, the claim was made that such policy makers were in the forefront of a mass movement propelling them forward. If, as was claimed, comprehensive reorganisation came about as a consequence of deep-seated social and economic forces, we may expect, therefore, it was an overwhelmingly popular movement. What, then, is the evidence?

Certainly it is not very powerful for George Tomlinson, who

replaced Ellen Wilkinson as Minister of Education in 1947. Tomlinson warned that 'the [Labour] Party are kidding themselves if they think that the comprehensive idea has any popular appeal' (quoted in Parkinson 1970, p. 47). In this warning Tomlinson was no doubt relying upon his common sense and his knowledge of opinion at the grass roots. In 1957, the Labour Party sought to increase their knowledge of such grass roots by commissioning a public opinion poll on attitudes to the reform of the educational system. According to Parkinson the poll suggested in general that 'the vast majority of the public were ignorant of the issues involved in comprehensive reorganisation' (1970, p. 81). On the specific question of selection – that aspect of secondary schooling considered to be the most unpopular – it seemed that 'only ten per cent of the sample, anyway, felt that segregated education was socially undesirable . . .' (Parkinson, p. 81). Summarising the results of the poll, Parkinson said: 'The majority of parents were basically satisfied with the existing education system, and, while there was a strong desire for traditional changes, such as the reduction of the size of classes, there was practically none for radical reorganisation.' (1970, p. 81.)

Ten years later in 1967, the findings of a poll, conducted by Research Service Limited and *New Society*, were reported in the journal of that name. David Donnison, then Professor of Social Administration, London School of Economics, and later from 1968 to become chairman of the Public Schools Commission, both presented and commented upon the findings of the poll (*New Society*, 26 October 1967). On the surface public opinion appeared to have turned about in favour of comprehensive (and therefore radical) reorganisation. In answer to the question 'Are you in favour or against comprehensive education?', of the sample of adults interviewed, 52 per cent were in favour. There was a majority of all 'social grades' in favour with the highest percentage against (37 per cent) in 'social grade' AB: professional and managerial interviewees. Nevertheless, the percentage of 'don't knows' was quite high: 29 per cent; and highest in 'social grade' DE (unskilled manual workers) at 38 per cent.

However, Donnison rightly spotted that caution was required in interpreting this finding in favour of comprehensive education. For 76 per cent of the sample (and this included, according to Donnison, 68 per cent of those in favour of the comprehensives) said that they were in favour of retaining grammar schooling. And 46 per cent would choose a grammar school as a place for their child, given that he was (hypothetically) acceptable to a variety of types of schools. In contrast, only 16 per cent chose a comprehensive school and a mere 10 per cent expressed a preference for the secondary modern. The grammar school thus remained the top of the poll. Professor Donnison refused to see anything odd in favouring comprehensive schools whilst preferring that one's own children are educated at a grammar school. Donnison argued: 'There is no contradiction in voting for the abolition of different passenger classes while preferring first-class travel so long as two classes remain.' (p. 585.) It was in this spirit, no doubt, that the one-time General Secretary of the British Communist Party, Harry Pollitt, sent one of his sons to Eton College as being the best school that British capitalism could provide. The logic is impeccable; but one cannot help wondering about the sincerity of a belief in some future and alternative system whilst such hard-headed use is being made of the best the present system can offer.

Perhaps there is, and was, no contradiction in believing that comprehensive schools are a good thing whilst not wishing to abolish grammar schools (and the necessity to select their pupils). The philosopher and noted educationalist, Mary Warnock, argued that 'there is every reason to believe that comprehensive schools are the best we could have. . . . Provided, then, that a system of comprehensive schools does not automatically deprive children of the right if necessary to be educated outside that system; and provided that, within the system, regard is given to the needs of children . . .' (Warnock, 1979, p. 40). It is, of course, provisions of this sort that the advocates of comprehensive schooling are most unwilling to supply.

Not only were respondents of the *New Society* poll willing to retain grammar schooling, but, in addition, there was a small majority in favour of retaining the much maligned eleven-plus; 46 per cent in favour of retention; 43 per cent against. A fair degree of ignorance seems to be shown by the sample interviewed. For example, a third had no idea whether or not their area had a system of comprehensive education; and 26 per cent did not know if, in their area, an eleven-plus system was in operation. It is, therefore, not very surprising to note that somewhat over half of the sample thought they needed to know more about educational matters.

Of those parents, who both had children in a comprehensive school *and* knew it to be such, 85 per cent were in favour of comprehensive schooling. As Donnison remarks this finding 'is all the more striking when it is remembered that most of these schools were not in the strictest sense comprehensive at all' (1967, p. 585). Rather more information on the attitudes of parents of children in comprehensive schools is to be found in a research report, *Progress in Secondary Schools: Findings from the National Child Development Study*. The report is of a research project which had 'its origins in a much longer-term study of all the people in Great Britain born in one week of March, 1958' (1980, p. 1). I will look at this report in greater detail in chapter 7; it suffices for the moment to say that the Department of Education and Science funded research between 1977–79 employing data collected by the National Child Development Study (NCDS) to evaluate 'aspects of progress in selective and non-selective schools'.

The findings concerned three types of school: comprehensive; grammar; and secondary modern. 'Of the three schooling groups,' the author of the report, Jane Steedman, wrote: 'pupils in comprehensives were "odd ones out", in that their parents were less likely to indicate satisfaction with their schooling.' (p. 193.) Jane Steedman attempts to quantify the differences in satisfaction: 'The odds of "selective" pupils having parents who indicate satisfaction with their schooling were nearly 2½ times the equivalent odds for children in purpose-built comprehensives.' . . . 'Purpose-built schools, moreover, were comprehensives associated with the highest level of parental satisfaction of all the 1969-or-earlier comprehensives' . . . 'the odds for [parental satisfaction in] the grammar modern group were well over 3½ times the odds that parents in former grammar schools would register satisfaction' (p. 194). On the other hand, the dissatisfaction that some parents registered is used also as a positive example, perhaps showing a bias in favour of comprehensive schooling within the report: 'it may be that indications of dissatisfaction reflect a certain criticality [*sic*] or involvement in decisions about schooling among parents which some schools would hope to foster' (p. 201).[7]

If we turn our attention from the findings of public opinion polls and social surveys, and look for enlightenment from seasoned observers, officials and practical politicians, the story is much the same. For instance, Rene Saran, in her case study of educational policy-making in a large urban local education authority, comments that: 'parental pressure was an important factor supporting the selective secondary schools structure in general and access, at public expense, to fee-paying schools in particular' (1973, p. 17). And writing specifically of attempts to reform the school system in the immediate post-war period, Saran claims that: 'In general the role of parents in the decisions studied was to defend the selective system. The only exception to this was parental support for the comprehensive school in an area where there was no grammar school.' (p. 263.) P. H. James, in a book summarising many case studies, *The Reorganization of Secondary*

Education, notes that in contrast to many objections to grammar school closures, and in reference to Saran's study: 'The only exception of parental support for comprehensive education was in an area notable for its lack of a grammar school. And even here parental protest later developed when it was discovered that children in this area would not be allowed to attempt the eleven-plus and opt for grammar instead of comprehensive schooling.' (1980, p. 43.) Writing in the late 1970s, Maurice Kogan, Professor of Government and Social Administration at Brunel University, and an important member of the educational establishment of the 1960s, rather sadly concludes that 'working-class parents' have not been 'the most fervent supporters of comprehensive education' (1978, p. 157).

Who then, did support comprehensive schooling? Headmaster Michael Hinton claimed that: 'The emotional impetus against the eleven-plus came largely from those parents – middle-class or with middle-class ambitions – who feared seeing their children condemned to working-class modern schools.' (1979, p. 32.) This opinion is strongly supported by an experienced chief education officer of Leeds, George Taylor, who, in a conversation with Professor Kogan published in *County Hall*, argued that: 'Pressure for comprehensive schools came from middle-class parents anxious that their children might not get selective education and therefore wanting to do away with the eleven-plus.' (1973, p. 172.) However much one might sympathise with such middle-class parents and their anxieties about their children, did they constitute a mass movement? And did they provide those strong motivations which were claimed to be the source of fundamental forces driving the bandwagon of comprehensive reorganisation? Such a group seems little more than a pressure group and amongst many such groups in modern society; and, hardly one which any self-respecting egalitarian might wish to align himself.

Given, then, such an absence of general public and parental support for the abolition of grammar schools and their replacement by comprehensive schools, it comes as no surprise to find that politicians and officials ignore (when they do not misinform) the public when schools are reorganised. Dan Cook, Chief Education Officer of Devon at the time of conversing with Professor Kogan and providing thus further material for *County Hall* (1973), commented both frankly and ingenuously '. . . I don't think that public opinion significantly affects the work and policy of a good local education authority, which should, in fact, be moulding opinion' (p. 91). James (1980) argues that studies of secondary reorganisation suggest: 'There was little evidence of members or officers attaching much importance to the need to take account of parental opinion.' (p. 118.) The conclusion must be that comprehensive reorganisation went ahead without the support (and often in defiance) of public and parental opinion.

Two further examples are enough to support such a conclusion. Following a decision in Liverpool to reorganise on comprehensive lines, a Liverpool Parents Protest Committee sprang up, and 32,000 signatures were collected that, under Section 13 of the 1944 Education Act, permitted an appeal to the Minister of Education on school closure. James notes 'the group was quite unable to succeed in exerting pressure directly on the LEA and whatever success it may have achieved was brought about indirectly' (1980, p. 49). In Bath, clearly a more enlightened authority, there was a civilised and 'an established tradition in the town of informed and involved discussion of locally controversial issues' (James, 1980, p. 50). The discussion of comprehensive reorganisation – a controversial issue *par excellence* – lead to public opposition to such a policy. Quite rightly, therefore, the Council rejected proposals for reorganisation – a decision condemned by a democratic local Labour Party education spokesperson as 'death by consultation' (quoted in James, 1980, p. 50). However, the story has a sadder sequel, for what James describes as 'a growing degree of political decisiveness and authority' (a euphemistic phrase for local tyranny?) enabled the LEA to ignore the expression of considered public opinion; and, 'the selectivists were not able to use again the consultative process to gather their forces and defeat proposals' (1980, p. 50).

Professional opinion on comprehensive reorganisation

If general and parental opinion was in favour of retaining grammar schools, and lukewarm about comprehensives, could the supporters of the latter look to teachers as their natural allies in reform?

A survey commissioned by *The Times Educational Supplement* and *The Times Higher Education Supplement* from National Opinion Polls may help to answer this question. The survey was carried out in the run-up to the October 1974 British general election. The survey sampled 1,173 teachers working in Britain and registered as voters. Some questions related to such professional matters as educational reform. The authors of a report on the survey, in interpreting its finding found surprising (as readers by now may not), 'the very small degree of support to be found across all shades of political opinion for the major educational reforms of the past decade – the move towards a comprehensive system of education and the raising of the school-leaving age. The vast majority, from all institutions and all parties, clearly thoroughly disapproved of both these measures.' (p. 3.)

In response to, for our purposes, the key statement: 'All grammar schools should be abolished', the report observes: 'An overwhelming majority (70 per cent) disagreed with the statement and can therefore be taken as being in favour of grammar schools.' (p. 19.) Whilst there is no wonder at the finding that only 6 per cent of teachers who were Conservative voters agreed with the statement, it is of more interest – because running counter to conventional expectations – that 37 per cent of those who were both teachers and Labour voters disagreed with the proposition clearly and unambiguously set out above. As the authors of the report put it, 'In other words, nearly two out of five Labour supporters were prepared to go against the party line on what is, for the Labour Party, a crucial education issue.' (p. 9.)

As an answer to the question set out at the beginning of this section all this is satisfactory enough. But it does prompt yet another question: Why did the teachers' professional organisation not more clearly articulate the opinions of their members?

There are at least two answers to this question. First, the position of the teachers' unions in relation to comprehensive reorganisation was not an easy one. A prime function of a union is the protection and promotion of its members' interests. Teachers do not form a united front here; but, rather, they are divided into a variety of unions large and small that in a rough and ready way mirror divisions within the teaching profession. There was no doubt that radical reform of the secondary school system was to have important consequences for the prospects and promotion of teachers. By the late 1950s, the teachers' unions had decided to concentrate on the protection of members' interests, rather than upon active opposition to secondary reorganisation. And besides, given the fragmented character of the teaching profession, the unions did not share the same interests. The Joint Four, representing the interests of university graduates teaching mainly in selective schools, had perhaps the most to lose: at least if the closure of grammar schools was of regret for its membership – which it probably was. On the other hand, experienced graduate teachers, no doubt, did spot the opportunities arising in the comprehensive schools for their graduate qualifications and the academic knowledge that they represented. The academic departments of the new comprehensives (and sixth-form colleges) were led and staffed by graduates from the grammar schools – with the consequences that some of the traditions of the grammar school were transplanted to the new stock of the comprehensive school. This was no bad thing, perhaps; but helped to ensure in the eyes of the more radical supporters of reorganisation that the comprehensive schools were that in name only.

In contrast, the National Union of Teachers, in so far as it represented mainly primary school teachers, was less directly affected by reorganisation – at least in terms of pay and promotion. The National Association of Schoolmasters (in 1976 to be linked with the Union of Women Teachers) represented non-graduate teachers: a number of whom were teaching in secondary schools. This latter group, in the immediate post-war years, feared that comprehensive reorganisation would limit their career opportunities. To some extent, this has been an accurate forecast as some LEAs restricted headships to graduates alone; and the prospects for promotion in the academic departments is more limited for the non-graduate. Such fears have, however, been alleviated to some degree. The great expansion in the late 1960s and early 1970s of secondary schooling, consequent upon increasing pupil numbers, provided opportunities for all – irrespective of initial qualifications. The establishment of the Open University in 1969, although intended as a kind of 'second-chance' university, became a means by which school teachers could achieve graduate status. The opportunity for gaining a degree part-time was taken by many non-graduate teachers; and, in addition, their numbers gave a measure of support and stimulus to the Open University itself.[8] Perhaps of even greater importance was the development in the comprehensive schools of pastoral and guidance systems (of which more anon), providing opportunities for employment, status, and promotion for the non-graduate (or the graduate qualified in some unconventional way).

For these reasons the unions acquiesced in comprehensive reorganisation, reserving instead their energy for the fight that took place in many LEAs over how the schools should be reformed. Here, the unions concentrated their attention on attempting to ensure that those members, whose careers were brought to a dead end by reorganisation, were properly recompensed; and also in demanding that salaries were 'safeguarded', so that reorganisation, whilst it might adversely affect the status of their members, would not cut their pay. On these matters LEAs agreed to give way. Such representations were the small change of local government policy-making; authorities were accustomed to buying their way out of trouble, without too much

concern for accurately costing reorganisation. This was a financial policy that could be followed until C. A. R. Crosland, as a
Labour Minister for the Environment, told an incredulous local
authority world, 'The party is over': words that have an increasingly prophetic ring about them. Another difficulty facing the
unions arose from the fact that their members were employees of
local councils. As such they could not stand for election to the
councils; although a handful of teachers are permitted, under the
1944 Education Act, to serve as co-opted members of education
committees. However, it is clear that many LEAs expected their
teachers, as their employees, to support council policy rather
than to subvert it. Teachers expressed disapproval or criticism of
policy at their peril. A striking example of the dangers of dissent
is to be found in Saran's *Policy-making in Secondary Education: a case
study.*

Saran provides a blow-by-blow account of an early attempt
(1948) at reorganisation in a local authority she rather coyly calls
'Townsley' (internal evidence so freely provided by Saran reveals
this LEA to be Middlesex). A local government election was to
take place in 1949; and, Saran suggests, the proximity of the
election prompted the Labour Party in power to rush through a
scheme of secondary reorganisation The consequence was that
'Many assistant teachers heard of the possible reorganisation of
their school through press advertisements in April (1948), followed by the letters of dismissal sent to headteachers.' (Saran,
1973, p. 151.) Part of the scheme involved the closure of a
grammar school. At a public meeting held to inform the public of
details of the proposed reorganisation, the grammar school head
was the first to speak against the scheme (perhaps with his letter
of dismissal in his pocket). Saran records that the party political
lady in the chair, and chairperson of the education committee,
condemned his speech as being 'inflammatory and extremely
foolish'. She followed this up by describing the headmaster as a
'servant' of the education committee. Saran reports that she
'further commented that "she was tired of employees of the
Council" – here she was interrupted by calls of "cheek!" – "using
their position to stir up opposition"' (Saran, 1973, p. 155).

This story has an ugly sequel. With a wealth of judicial
wisdom, rivalling the Court of Appeal in Ordinary, a local
secretary of the NUT adjudicated that: 'the headmaster's speech
was against the common law, which requires a public servant to
refrain from acting against the interest of his master' (quoted in
Saran, 1973, p. 156). Saran reports: 'The headmaster was, in fact,
severely disciplined by the Chief Education Officer and almost
lost his job' and further: 'the Council adopted a standing order

that no officer was permitted to act against the policy of the council' (p. 156).

In the light of the above, it was understandably prudent (following Middlesex's attempt to reorganise) that the 'teacher groups' response to reorganisation became more and more sectional reflecting the traditional divisions within English education' (James, 1980, p. 55). Nevertheless, as James records, teachers' unions were still prepared to oppose comprehensive reorganisation in the 1950s. In 1954, the NAS passed an Annual Conference resolution 'to the effect that there was not yet sufficient evidence to justify the widespread establishment of comprehensive schools' (p. 55). And again in 1954, the NUT 'opposed further comprehensive experiments until the existing ones were proved satisfactory' (p. 56). But by 1964 (perhaps with thought of the consequences of a new-broom Labour administration in power) James points out that 'the NUT was co-operating with the Joint Four in producing a common statement which was concerned with procedures for consultation and not with arguing the case for or against reorganisation' (p. 56).

The conclusion is that LEAs were as unwilling to discuss and to consult with teachers over their plans for secondary reorganisation as they were with the general public and parents. In so far as LEAs did make such an attempt, according to Ribbins and Brown, in an article summarising such procedures, 'the object of the exercise was more to solicit agreement (and therefore commitment) from teachers, or else to show that teachers were divided (which they mostly were) on the issue involved' (1979, p. 194). Perhaps in all this the LEAs were only being honest, for in the words of Margaret Thatcher: 'consultation is only meaningful when you intend to be influenced by the representations' (quoted in James, 1980, p. 80).

Of course some teachers were strongly in favour of comprehensive reorganisation – often on ideological grounds. The National Association of Labour Teachers and the Socialist Educational Association were important pressure groups within the Labour Party, encouraging it to accept proposals for comprehensive reorganisation. James noted in addition that: 'Quite small numbers of teachers, as members of local Labour Parties, had on occasions a very considerable influence [*sic*] promoting the comprehensive school.' (1980, p. 69.) Such groups of teachers applied similar pressure within the teachers' unions. According to Fenwick 'Middlesex Teachers' Association consistently submitted motions for debate by the NUT annual conferences, pledging support for comprehensive schools . . .'. (1976, p. 46.) Fenwick also claims that 'some of the most vocal supporters of the comprehensive school at the national level came from the Middlesex Association and it had also a very active group of Communist and left-wing Socialist members' (p. 46). Indeed Fenwick argues, with respect to the NUT, that 'the political driving force behind the comprehensive school lobby was diminished when, in 1949, the Communists in office in the union were defeated after an internal union quarrel' (p. 69).

In the 1960s, such groups of teachers coalesced with university dons, college lecturers, politicians, and ideologists of one type or another, to form influential pressure groups. In 1960, the Association for the Advancement of State Education (ACE) was formed in Cambridge by parents presumably wishing to promote the end suggested by the title of their organisation. This organisation was later to promote *Where*, a journal comparable in some respects to *Which*, in so far as it attempts to create a better informed (and, therefore, more choosey) clientele for state education. ACE was later to have an offshoot, the Campaign for the Advancement of State Education (CASE) whose members in part were a pressure group for comprehensive reorganisation. James, indeed, noted that 'In general, local branches of CASE have exerted pressure in favour of comprehensive schools providing both a monitoring system and actively lobbying councillors and disseminating information which supports the comprehensive ideal.' (1980, p. 44.) More exclusively concerned with the reform of secondary schools was the Comprehensive Schools Committee, founded in 1965, and whose membership overlapped with ACE and CASE. This committee regularly published *Comprehensive Education*, which along with *Forum*, first published in autumn 1958, were the main journals of the comprehensive school lobby. These journals obviously had a propaganda function, but they also provided a mass of information as to how LEAs were going comprehensive in different parts of the country. This information was not easily found elsewhere; so the journals became almost indispensable to those educational journalists who were recruited by most newspapers (and some weeklies) in the 1960s: a sign, perhaps, of increasing public concern and interest in education.

The officers and editors of these organisations overlapped. Professors Pedley and Simon edited *Forum*; Caroline Benn (wife to Anthony Wedgwood Benn) a graduate of that highly esteemed American institution, Vassar College, was Information Officer for the Comprehensive Schools Committee (from 1972, for the National Campaign for Comprehensive Education), and editor of *Comprehensive Education*. She performed the important task of collecting and collating information as to how British LEAs were going comprehensive. There is, then, considerable evidence to support Professor Kogan in his claim that in the 1960s 'a new educational Establishment' (of which he was a member) developed (see Kogan, 1971, p. 46). Very much later in 1981, the members of the 'Education Group', who compiled a critique of what they describe as the social democratic policies of the 1960s entitled *Unpopular Education*, observed: 'A few selected "experts" gained privileged access to powerful personnel in the Labour Party and in the state, and were thus able to influence considerably the politics of schooling from the top downwards.' (1981, p. 244.)

The politics of reorganisation

There is no evidence, then, that there was widespread support for comprehensive reorganisation amongst the general public, parents, or teachers. Indeed, the drive towards comprehensive reform was against much professional advice; as Belski notes: 'the general climate of opinion of educationalists and administrators favoured the tripartite system' (1973, p. 202). How, therefore, did such a momentous reform take place?

To answer this question we must consider the way that British schools are politically controlled. The state has almost total control over education – and many comprehensive school supporters want this control to be absolute. In effect this puts the control of schools, and potentially the curriculum, in the hands of national and local politicians. The control of schooling rests in parliament, and in town and county halls up and down the country. There is evidence, however, that education is not a matter of great importance to politicians and political parties.

Political parties are more interested in economic matters; law and order; and perhaps in the case of the Conservative Party, foreign affairs. Secretaries of State for Education are not regarded as being major ministers of the Crown, in the way that we consider the Chancellor of the Exchequer, the Foreign Secretary and the Home Secretary, very important personages. Sometimes education ministers are not members of the Cabinet. This means that they are not considered important enough to take part in discussion of government policy; nor can such excluded ministers so readily argue the case for education (and resources for it).

This low ordering of education may, in a rough and ready way, reflect the opinion of the nation. Most people look to government to secure economic wellbeing – however that is interpreted – and national security, rather than reform of the educational system. For this reason, it is probably unwise to see in the swings and pendulums of party political fortune some clue to the nation's views on secondary school reform. Nevertheless, it is the politicians who, through parliament and town hall, control the schools and may decide on how they are to be organised.

In the immediate post-war years, there is no evidence that politicians of either of the two main parties, at national or local level, wished radically to reorganise the schools. Ellen Wilkinson was the first Labour Minister of Education in the Attlee post-war administration. She was thought to be something of a radical – perhaps because she helped to lead the famous Jarrow crusade. However, she made it clear that she had no intention of abolishing the grammar schools and the selective system necessary for their survival. Fenwick quotes Wilkinson as stating it was not her intention 'to destroy the grammar schools. . . . It would be folly to injure them.' (1976, p. 54.) And in both defence and explanation of Ellen Wilkinson's readiness to defend the grammar school, Betty Vernon in her biography, *Ellen Wilkinson 1891–1947* (1982), states that: 'there was no groundswell of enthusiasm for multi-lateralism within the Labour Party as a whole' (p. 217). Indeed, Ellen Wilkinson regarded the provision of one third of a pint of milk free to all pupils under eighteen 'as a culmination of our promise [the Labour Party's] to do away with class distinction.' A point she re-emphasised at the 1946 Labour Party conference where she said: 'Free milk will be provided in Hoxton and Shoreditch, in Eton and Harrow. What more social equality can you have than that?' (quoted in Vernon (1982) p. 214.)

Wilkinson's successor in office, George Tomlinson, held simlar views. Fenwick points out that 'The new minister went out of his way, in the 1947 debate on the education vote, to emphasise "that it is no part of our policy to reduce in any way the status or standing of the grammar school"' (1976, p. 57). Fenwick (1976) claims that in the Attlee government no more than half a dozen Labour MPs supported comprehensive schools.

Nor were local authorities any more interested in abolishing grammar schools and replacing them by comprehensives. As Fenwick remarks, 'few local authorities, even among those that were Labour controlled were convinced of the viability of the comprehensive school' (1976, p. 60). As late as 1973, the Chief Education Officer for Leeds, George Taylor, in conversation with Professor Kogan claimed that 'Until comparatively recently, the Labour Party in local authorities had little enthusiasm for comprehensive schools . . .' (Kogan, 1973, p. 171). For as Saran points out, 'in Labour ranks, as elsewhere, there were staunch supporters of the grammar school, who often defended these schools as an avenue for talented working-class children to make good' (1973, p. 124). Indeed it is noteworthy that in County Durham, a

Labour stronghold since 1919 (and the first local authority in Britain to be controlled by the Labour Party), did not go comprehensive until after the passing of the 1976 Education Act compelling local authorities so to do.

It is true that some proposals for organising the schools on comprehensive lines were proposed by a handful of local authorities. Anglesey in the north of Wales, sparsely populated and rural, found it difficult, given the scattered character of its small population, to create a selective system. For reasons, then, that were wholly pragmatic, and without any concern to fulfil an egalitarian ideal, it organised its schools on comprehensive lines with the backing of the Ministry of Education. Proposals put forward from the London County Council (LCC) and Middlesex, as we have seen, were in contrast ideologically motivated. Even here, despite that declared opinion of the Labour government in favour of grammar schools and a selective system, such schemes were not rejected outright. In this the Minister of Education was only following the 1944 Education Act. The law did not dictate the form of secondary organisation, and so long as the plans and behaviour of LEAs were 'reasonable', and the LEAs provided 'efficient instruction' sufficient for the diverse abilities, ages and aptitudes of children, central government could not veto LEA proposals. However, in the case of the plans proposed by Middlesex, a Labour Minister of Education did not find them 'reasonable' enough and they were in part rejected. Indeed, in Middlesex, the Ministry of Education wished to be assured that the plans to close grammar schools met with the general wishes of parents and public (a stipulation that the LEA did not make generally known until much of the controversy was over). And it took three years for the ministry to approve the plans of the LCC to create some comprehensive schools.

The 1950s saw some changes in the attitudes of the two main political parties. The greatest were within the Labour Party. This Party can be said to be divided into two parts. That is between those that believe in socialism and see the Party as a means of creating a socialist state and society; and those, although reluctantly prepared to pay lip service to such an ideal (in the way that the leaders of the Party sing the Red Flag in a self-conscious and embarrassed way at the end of Party Conferences), that if they believe in anything, it is in the virtues of a mixed economy. This latter group is and was made up of professional politicians, seasoned by office, and more sharply aware than constituency activists of a wider public outside the narrow confines of the party itself. In opposition, the radicals play a larger role than when the Party is in office. For thirteen years, from 1951 to 1964, the Labour

Party was in exile. In those years, despite the abortive attempts of Hugh Gaitskell, the leader throughout many years of opposition, to reshape the constitution and policies of the Party to what he believed to be its truer inclination, some radical and socialist policies became officially accepted. Amongst those measures were the proposals to create a comprehensive system of education and to do something or other about private education. The annual Party Conference was crucial to this change in Labour Party policy.

The fiction or myth within the Labour Party is that conference determines the policy of the Party: to be implemented whenever and wherever the Party is in power. As that staunch parliamentarian and Labour leader, Michael Foot, has pointed out, conference decisions are frequently too vague to be useful; contradictory; sometimes reversed by a succeeding conference; and are managed by a compositing committee who join together constituency resolutions. Such resolutions are then largely approved or disapproved by union block votes with little reference to the actual size of the rather nominal Labour Party support within their unions. Experienced Labour leaders no doubt regarded the decisions of Labour Party conferences as the politicians in Ancient Greece regarded the findings of the Delphic oracle: to be used or ignored as they chose.

Within the conference, the National Association of Labour Teachers annually urged the acceptance of the comprehensive principle. Amongst MPs, Alice Bacon was a worthy protagonist in the cause of abolishing grammar schools. An example of her rhetoric is provided by Fenwick, who quotes her as saying at the 1953 conference: 'Mr and Mrs Brown, the ordinary parents of this country, do not feel aggrieved because their Tommy goes to a council school whilst little Lord Pantalduke goes to Eton; but what does grieve them is that Jimmy Jones over the road has a scholarship to the grammar school while their Tommy has to stay in the modern school.' (1976, p. 78.) It might be difficult to find anywhere a statement which both encourages and imputes envy of the most petty kind to the parents of children at secondary moderns. Grammar schools are to be destroyed because everyone cannot attend them. It might also be noted that from Alice Bacon's envious point of view the larger injustice – the existence of schools such as Eton – must be considered a lesser matter because such schools are beyond the ken of the likes of Mr and Mrs Brown.

In an appeal to such feelings of envy believed to be widespread, a report (1953) of the National Executive of the Labour Party (NEC) argued that: 'Not only does Socialist principle demand it . . . [but] . . . electorally a policy which showed how to do away with the gross inequality of the present school system could win a great deal of popularity.' (quoted in Parkinson, 1970, p. 72.) The belief that such a policy would have electoral support was shattered by the findings of the NOP poll commissioned by the Labour Party four years later in 1957. From then onwards the emphasis was less on the inequalities of the selective system, and rather more on the policy of promoting grammar schools for all. Indeed, Hugh Gaitskell, the Labour leader, went so far as to 'describe our proposals [the Labour Party's] as "a grammar school education for all".' (Gaitskell's letter to *The Times*, 5 July 1958 quoted in Fenwick, 1976, p. 109.) This misdescription of his own party's education policy was repeated (to the embarrassment of his more authentically socialist colleagues and followers) by Harold Wilson in the run-up to the 1964 general election. In a study of the Labour Party's education policy Parkinson suggests that there was a degree of equivocation in its presentation of the comprehensive principle. The Party played down the allegedly unjust and socially divisive character of the selective system, and suggested rather (as in Harold Wilson's 'Science and Socialism' speech to the 1963 conference) that it 'held back Britain's technological development and operated against our success in economic affairs' (Parkinson, 1970, p. 88).

The eagerness of the Labour Party to abolish grammar schools (whilst retaining grammar school education) was not matched by a similar zeal to rid Britain of its public schools. Parkinson quotes from a 1956 Labour Party memorandum 'designed to summarise and crystallise the Party's general position on private education: ". . . to abolish private education altogether would be physically and administratively difficult and it is doubtful whether it can be ethically justified in a democratic society"' (1970, p. 111). The paradox (or is it contradiction?) of advocating the abolition of grammar schools (the major channel of advancement and self-fulfillment for working-class boys and girls) whilst at the same time, however reluctantly, holding back from destroying those schools allegedly benefiting only the most gilded youth, was not lost on 'Manny' Shinwell, the elder statesman of Labour leaders.[9] In a letter to *The Times* that was to prompt a response from Hugh Gatskell (a fragment from which is quoted above) Shinwell argued:

> We are afraid to tackle the public schools to which the wealthy people send their sons, but at the same time are ready to throw overboard the grammar schools, which are for many working-class boys the stepping stones to the

universities and a useful career – I would rather abandon Eton, Winchester, Harrow and all the rest of them than sacrifice the advantage of the grammar school. (*The Times*, 26 June 1958).

Why did the Labour Party leaders accept as Party policy a reform of secondary schooling about which they had so many doubts and reservations? One explanation is that at a time of discord between the various factions of the Party over economics, defence and foreign policy 'the leadership was prepared to buy rank and file loyalty in the more important areas by yielding in the traditionally less important area of education' (Fenwick, 1976, p. 157).

The years of Conservative Party rule, 1951–1964, were not a period of dogmatic and authoritarian opposition to comprehensive schools. However, as Fenwick (1976, p. 103) put it, there was 'a definite commitment to the preservation and extension of the grammar schools' – a policy which seemed to do consecutive Conservative administrations no electoral harm whatsoever. Fenwick notes that neither Florence Horsborough nor David Eccles, as ministers of education, were outright opponents of comprehensive schools; indeed, Fenwick quotes Eccles as saying he would consider proposals for 'comprehensive schools on their merits' (1976, p. 73). Again ministers, no doubt, considered that their response to the few proposals for the establishment of comprehensive schools that came their way, could not, under the 1944 Education Act, be one of outright rejection. Where such proposals did not involve the closure of a grammar school – or indeed the rights of parents to enter their children as candidates for such schools – the plans might be approved. Thus, ministry policy did not positively discourage the creation of comprehensive schools on (say) large local authority housing estates where no grammar schools existed. Whether such tolerance indicated an indifference to the fate of children on such estates who may well have benefited from grammar school education of a traditional kind is a matter of debate. Until the publishing of Circular 10/65, however, it is fair to say that both Labour and Conservative governments had opposed 'any widespread introduction of comprehensive schools, focussing mainly on the difficulties associated with size and the threat they posed to existing grammar schools.' (James, 1980, p. 26.)

The election in 1964 brought the Labour Party to power; and now officially committed to comprehensive reorganisation, it changed all that. Crosland, in 1956, had written 'there can be no question of suddenly closing down the grammar schools and

converting the secondary moderns into comprehensive schools.'
And further: 'Until and unless the proper supply conditions
exist, it would be quite wrong to close down grammar schools of
acknowledged academic quality.' (p. 275.) It is to Crosland's
credit that he as a minister did not wholly abandon this earlier
view; and decided that because the way ahead was 'studded with
obstacles, the shortage of public buildings, the state of public
opinion, and the fact of local self-determination, comprehensive
reorganisation would be introduced at a moderate pace' (quoted
in Parkinson, 1970, p. 89).

For this reason, legislation was not thought to be wise ('the
state of public opinion', etc.); and, instead, it was rule by circular
instead. Circular 10/65 (12 July 1965) was sent to LEAs, the
Governors of Direct Grant, Voluntary Aided and Special Agreement Schools. They were informed it was the government's
declared objective 'to end selection at eleven-plus and to eliminate separation in secondary education' by amongst other things
preserving 'all that is valuable in grammar school education for
those children who now receive it and to make it available to more
children . . .'. How 'separation in education' was to be eliminated
was not all that clear; at least six main forms of comprehensive
organisation had so far emerged, the Circular pointed out. The
Circular was a request that LEAs submit plans for the reorganisation of secondary education on comprehensive lines (however
ill-defined such lines might be). The Circular pointed out that:
'The smooth inception and continuing success of any scheme of
reorganisation will depend on the co-operation of teachers and
the support and confidence of parents. To secure these there
must be a process of consultation and explanation . . .' (para. 40).
The Circular spoke of 'close and genuine consultation with
teachers'; whilst with parents it was important only 'that they
should be informed fully and authoritatively as soon as practicable in the planning stage' (para. 42). On the important question
of resources to support such a momentous reform the Circular
points out that LEAs would receive no financial assistance simply
for the purposes of reorganisation (so much for the 'proper
supply conditions' without which 'it would be quite wrong to
close down grammar schools of acknowledged academic quality'). As Benn and Simon remark: 'Undoubtedly a definite
commitment of resources for reorganisation should certainly
have been part of the policy of any government seriously bent on
a major reform of this nature . . .' (1970, p. 50).

Circular 10/65, although not a piece of education legislation
which had passed through the process of debate and discussion
in two houses of parliament, was an influential document. It was

an official declaration that central government, through the DES, was going to bring about a major reform of the secondary school system. Although LEAs who had no wish to go comprehensive could not be legally forced to, nevertheless, the power of the DES to control the LEAs' capital expenditure was a useful weapon. From 1966, the DES sanctioned loans to LEAs for capital expenditure (to be used, for example, in building or extending schools) on secondary schools only so long as they were comprehensive.

Along with such financial control, Circular 10/65 itself was important as giving the backing of government to reform in a very forceful way. James (1980) provides several examples of LEAs, previously content with the organisation of their secondary schooling, that were led to re-think and re-plan. James points out, for example, 'the majority Labour Party in Southampton was proud of that authority's selective system and did not seriously consider reorganisation until 10/65 was issued.' Indeed, he claims that 'the Labour controlled Birmingham council had until 1965 not been sufficiently convinced of the merits of comprehensive education to even seriously consider dismantling their selective system.' James argues that in this case, 'The decisive impetus . . . was therefore 10/65'. He suggests that Birmingham as the largest borough in the country and, to boot, Labour controlled, was looked on to set an example for all LEAs. The only alternative to going comprehensive was defying the Labour government – which for a Labour local authority was not a serious choice. As James records, 'whereas in the March of 1965 the Labour Group had rejected a comprehensive proposal, by December it had itself produced just such a plan' (p. 29).

Where Birmingham led, the nation followed. The return to power of the Conservatives in 1970 and later in 1979, made little difference. The bandwagon of comprehensive reform was rolling, and it had developed so much momentum it was well-nigh impossible to stop – despite Circular 10/70, returning control of education rather more to LEAs, and the repeal of the 1976 Education Act.

What, perhaps, is of further interest in this brief outline of how Britain went comprehensive is the manner of it. Plans were drawn up, and secondary systems reorganised with an astonishing absence of concern for public opinion and professional know-how. Ribbins and Brown (1979), in a survey of case-studies on secondary reorganisation, point out that 'general policy making in almost all areas of local authority activity is concentrated among the few . . . reorganisation is seen as a particularly complicated issue and most elected members are only too grateful to leave the effort of understanding it in any depth to a few party experts' (p. 191).

I have already outlined the fashion by which public and professional views were rarely considered (contrary, at any rate, as far as teachers are concerned to advice given in Circular 10/65). What is fascinating – given the claims made that comprehensive reorganisation was a popular movement and democratically supported – is how few people even within the dominant political party were involved. James, in his summary of case-studies of secondary reorganisation, provided instance after instance of how LEA policy was shaped by one or two individuals. In some LEAs they might be a dominant councillor; in other LEAs a chief education officer was the prime mover. Participation and consultation were at a minimum: often regarded as wholly time-wasting and futile on the part of elected members and officers alike. For example, Batley, *et al*, in their *Going Comprehensive* (1970), writing of secondary reorganisation in Gateshead and Darlington, note: 'The machinery of consultation seems, in both towns, to have been valuable as a pill sweetener. But it is hard to detect any point where the plans finally adopted were modified by the advice given.' (p. 98.)

The evidence on how Britain went comprehensive in the 1960s and 1970s points one way: that it was not a popular movement, but one that was encouraged, perhaps half-heartedly, by Labour governments, whilst pursued more tenaciously and doggedly by a remarkable handful of energetic politicians and administrators within the local authorities. The general public, parents and teachers were largely ignored. One wonders how educational historians such as Rubinstein and Simon can describe the re-organisation of secondary education as taking 'shape without the support of any of the major parties' in the light of evidence which had accummulated even by 1973. As for such a reform being a reflection of 'deep-seated economic and social changes' (1973, p. 119); if anything, comprehensive reform has attempted to defy social and economic tendencies: as we shall see more clearly in the following chapter.

4 Creating the system

'The selective school gets more selective, the comprehensives get less selective. That is the law of coexistence.' Caroline Benn, 1976.

10/65 and all that

It was one thing for the local politicians to abolish most or all of the maintained grammar schools in their authorities, and to dismantle the selective system. It was yet another thing by so doing to create comprehensive schools.

As noted in chapter 1, official educational statistics classify a school 'as comprehensive when its admission arrangements are without reference to ability and aptitude'. And the 1976 Education Act (now repealed) states as the comprehensive principle to be observed by all LEAs that secondary education 'is to be provided only in schools where the arrangements for the admission of pupils are not based (wholly or partly) on selection by ability and aptitude' (preamble to the Act). LEAs could follow these definitions and prescriptions to the letter, and yet fail to satisfy the demands of comprehensive reformers. I have already noted (chapter 1) how Professor Pedley deplores the decision, by the DES and the LEAs, to define as 'comprehensive' schools which by virtue of failing to attract 'the most able children in their community' (who prefer a nearby selective school), 'are little more than secondary moderns' (1978, p. 13). And Michael Hinton wrote of the non-selective secondary schools: 'Many of them are not even comprehensive in any meaningful sense of the word.' (1979, p. 1.) Such comments provide a sharp reminder that abandoning selection by reference to ability or aptitude is not enough in itself to create comprehensive schools and a comprehensive system.

Circular 10/65, *The Organization of Secondary Education*, stated that there are six main forms of comprehensive school – suggest-

61

ing thereby a degree of uncertainty about quite what precise shape and form a comprehensive school should take beyond that fact that it must not select. In the Circular, the 'orthodox comprehensive school' was described as one with an age range of eleven to eighteen (para. 6). The difficulty with this school was its size, which largely rested upon estimated numbers in the sixth form. If we assume that (as do many LEAs) a school requires 200 or more pupils in its sixth form (to provide enough pupils for a fair range of 'A' level courses, and other courses of a different and perhaps non-academic character); then, with a staying-on rate in the fifth year of one-third (this is considerably higher than is found in many schools) a lower school of some 1,650 children (eleven-form entry) is necessary, making a school of 1,870 pupils in all. The sixth form of this school contains only 220 pupils, and the staying-on rate is high. If more pupils are thought necessary for the sixth form, and/or the staying-on rate is lower than one-third, then the lower school will require to be proportionately larger.

Whether or not large schools are a good thing in themselves is a matter to be considered in the next chapter. As far as secondary reorganisation is concerned, such schools were thought to necessitate special buildings to house them. Such buildings required: very large assembly halls; gymnasia; dining rooms and kitchens, science, arts, handicrafts, and domestic science blocks; administrative suites to accommodate senior staff and their secretarial assistants; medical and restrooms; common rooms for staff and pupils; pastoral units and offices; libraries; playing fields covering several acres with special athletic training areas; and car parks serviced by roads and walkways. Not very surprisingly, few such schools were built. Those that were built are often referred to as 'show places'.

Circular 10/65 recommended that the 'all-through comprehensive' should be adopted 'whenever circumstances permitted' as 'the simplest and best solution' (para. 6). However, it was admitted: 'In practice . . . circumstances will usually not permit . . .' (para. 7); principally because most post-war schools were too small to be used as 11–18 comprehensives. Indeed, the Circular frankly conceded: 'The disposition, character and size of existing schools . . . must influence and in many cases go far to determine the shape of secondary organisation' (para. 23). Nor were LEAs permitted extra funds above and beyond that necessary to house their existing and increasing school populations.

As noted in chapter one, many LEAs, out of necessity, created 11–18 schools by linking together schools designed and built for quite different purposes. Schools, often miles apart, were brought together to form a single unit. In the split-site school, teachers and pupils spend a fair portion of their school time moving from one site to another. This may be tiresome enough in fine weather; in winter's snow, hail and rain, it becomes a more positive disadvantage. Schools, of course, have made valiant efforts of organisation to cope with the difficulties of split-site schools. Some, in effect, became two schools, with a lower school run by a deputy headteacher. But even in these circumstances, specialist staff may have to move from one site to another several times in a week. In addition, such schemes may have helped to undermine the attempts of teachers to maintain good order and discipline.

Circular 10/65 was aware of the limitations of split-site schools: 'If buildings are at a considerable distance from each other, or separated by busy roads, the disadvantages are obvious. Even when they are close together the amount and type of accommodation available may cause groupings of pupils which are arbitrary and educationally inefficient' (para. 8). Nevertheless, a member of Her Majesty's Inspectorate, in a paper, 'Patterns of Secondary Organisation' (DES, 1978), comments, in a reference to reorganisation following 10/65, 'Split sites were unavoidable at this time in many areas.' (DES, 1978, p. 1.) The anonymous Inspector argues plausibly enough: 'split sites may, in principle, seem to impose handicaps' (p. 4). And in a brave and loyal effort to rescue something from the wreckage, the Inspector sees some benefits nevertheless for 'a very large school to be broken down into more manageable units'; and that this can be of especial value 'in schools with an abnormal burden of social problems' (p. 4). This defence, however, does prompt at least one question. If small units are of especial value in coping with social problems, why create schools of unmanageable size in the first place? But HMIs are not expected to ask such awkward (and simple) questions: at least not in public.

Many local authorities, in view of the difficulties, did not attempt to establish the 'orthodox comprehensive school'. Instead, LEAs used what secondary school buildings were available to create a variety of 'two-tier systems'. These were acceptable as possible solutions to going comprehensive in Circular 10/65 with certain reservations. A two-tier system 'whereby *all* pupils transfer at 11 to a junior comprehensive school and *all* go on at 13 or 14 to a senior comprehensive school' (para. 3) was acceptable to the DES as being 'fully comprehensive in character'. Nevertheless, such a solution, it was recognised, was not without its limitations. Circular 10/65 points out that such schemes may 'produce problems of organisation' (para. 10). These include the necessity for schools 'to co-operate fully and positively in the choice of curriculum, syllabus and teaching method' (para. 10). The Circular recognised that the demands of such co-operation may limit the freedom of schools to develop in their own idiosyncratic ways. In addition, such schemes meant that for those children – the majority – who left school at fifteen, they would spend only two years in at least one of the schools. In addition, the difficulties of co-ordinating syllabuses was seen to be perhaps greatest for those following GCE courses in (say) mathematics, where continuity of teaching and learning is important. Finally, it is suggested in the Circular that such schemes, although to be considered 'fully comprehensive in character', may still be interim in so far as they may 'develop into an all-through system of orthodox comprehensive schools in the course of time as new buildings become available' (para. 10).

Not accepted as fully comprehensive schemes were those two-tier systems where children did not automatically move on to the senior school at the age of thirteen or fourteen. For such arrangements involved the deplorable 'separation of children of differing aims and aptitudes into different schools at the age of 13 or 14' (para. 4). These schemes could only be accepted 'as an interim stage in development towards a fully comprehensive secondary organisation' (para. 4). Professor Pedley in *The Comprehensive School* (1978) gives an account of the 'Leicestershire Scheme' which he helped to devise. In the 1950s, the secondary moderns of Leicestershire were transformed into junior comprehensives providing three-year courses. On completion of these courses, children could either remain or move to the senior comprehensive schools which, as Pedley admits, were the old unreconstituted grammar schools under a new name. There was no selection for the senior schools, but parents had to agree to keep their children at the schools for at least two years – to age sixteen. This became known as an option transfer system.

Pedley is well aware of all its disadvantages. The senior school 'would be neither a selective school for academic pupils nor a proper senior school' (1978, p. 52). In addition, such schemes favoured those middle-class parents who were willing to promise to keep their children in the senior schools until they were at least sixteen. What were then the advantages to Pedley of this scheme? First, it did away with the eleven-plus (although replacing it with parental choice at fourteen). And second, 'It would be a step on the way to a still better system.' (Pedley, 1978, p. 53.) A case of making things worse with the hope of making them better. A number of authorities 'experimented' with such a scheme in the wake of 10/65.

The Circular suggested two further approaches. One was the

11–16 school with transfer to a sixth-form college. In the 1960s, sixth-form colleges were a novelty, and the Circular simply debates their pros and cons whilst agreeing a limited number of experiments may be justified. Today, when such colleges threaten to provide the only opportunity for sixth-form work, they require a fuller consideration which I shall delay until chapter 7.

The final system, considered remotely comprehensive in character, involved the creation of middle schools straddling the primary/secondary age ranges. In 1965, the creation of such schools required special legislation, and were not easily created by LEAs (and perhaps not then) until the 1967 Education Act which gave them permission to do so. The middle schools created were intended to marry the then fashionable Plowden progressivism of the primary school with something of the more specialist approach of the secondary school. In retrospect it is difficult to judge their success. A number of authorities developed such schools, but with falling school rolls their numbers appear to be declining. Perhaps the division of British education at the age of eleven has been too deeply rooted for such schools to have much opportunity for development. Indeed, a recent report, *Schooling for the Middle Years* (1982) by Taylor and Garson, suggests that: 'One can hardly justify a system whose internal goals are to provide a smooth transition [from primary to secondary schooling] while externally the gap remains as wide as ever' (quoted in *The TES*, 1982 p. 21). The authors conclude an article, summarising their report, by pointing out that: 'Middle Schools were brought about by pressures external to the middle years of schooling' (*The TES*, 1982 p. 21).

The response of the LEAs to Circular 10/65 in the long run was to create, in the already quoted words of Caroline Benn and Brian Simon, schemes of reorganisation that were 'bewilderingly various from area to area'. The 1972 Local Government Act helped to compound the confusion by redrawing LEA boundaries at a time when many of them were trying to put their reorganisation plans into operation. The comments of an anonymous HMI therefore come as no surprise:

There is not only variety between different local authorities; within the same authority the pattern may vary with different ages of transfer operating in particular areas. Accordingly the type of school attended by a pupil of secondary age may depend on where he or she lives and to move from one area to another carries no assurance of similar school provision. (DES, 1978, p. 1.)

And so emerged the chaotic pattern of comprehensive reorganisation presented in outline in chapter 1. As Rubinstein and Simon put it with unconscious irony: 'The system now coming into being bore little resemblance, in some important respects, to early ideas as to comprehensive reorganisation – and even to the proposals in Circular 10/65.' (1973, p. 114.) But perhaps we can leave it to Professor Pedley to provide a verdict on a school system he has been instrumental in promoting: 'On a compact island with an increasingly mobile population, we cannot afford to have discrepancies between districts in the organisation of our educational system.' (1978, p. 56.)

Schools and their catchment areas

In *The Future of Socialism*, C. A. R. Crosland recommended that a future Labour government (in which he was, as things turned out, Secretary of State for Education) should 'actively encourage local authorities . . . to be more audacious in experimenting with comprehensive schools . . .'. However, at the bottom of that very page in a footnote to this recommendation, Crosland observes: 'But with the important proviso, in large cities which are divided into rather clearly-marked one-class neighbourhoods that the catchment areas are so drawn as to straddle neighbourhoods of different social standing.' (1956, p. 275.)

This footnote marks a realisation by Crosland that the abolition of selection was not enough in itself to guarantee comprehensive schools. Such schools, after all, were intended to be comprehensive in more than name. As Michael Hinton puts it, 'A comprehensive school is by definition a school designed for every level of ability and every kind of educational need.' (1979, p. 54.) Therefore, a comprehensive school should contain pupils of a full range of ability and from a variety of social backgrounds. In one school, then, will be found children of the highest intelligence and ability rubbing shoulders with those of the least. Children from all the races and religions found in the British isles will be integrated into one common or comprehensive school. That, at least, is the ideal. To quote Hinton again: 'a state school is more properly a microcosm of society than an extension of a sub-culture' (1979, p. 54). For this reason in Circular 10/65: 'The Secretary of State [Crosland in 1965] therefore urges authorities to ensure, when determining catchment areas, that schools are as socially and intellectually comprehensive as *is practicable*.' (para.

36, my italics.) But, how far *in practice* can schools be 'socially and intellectually comprehensive'?

The limitations of this catchment area policy were clearly foreseen and forecast by George Taylor, then Chief Education Officer for Leeds, in an article in the journal *New Society* (1 July 1965). He began with a reference to efforts so far: 'The Inner London Education Authority has made strenuous efforts to ensure that most of its comprehensive schools cater for a complete range of ability but it has been unable to arrange for a complete social cross-section to be represented in all its schools.' (p. 15.) Taylor went on to consider a hypothetical exercise of going comprehensive in the northern part of Leeds – presumably well-known to Taylor, and some 20,000 acres in area.

To house the pupils in the area, Taylor argued, 9 purpose-built schools with an eleven-form entry (the all-through orthodox comprehensive) would be required. In the area covered by the schools, school A would be six miles from schools E and F: 'it is, therefore, impossible to contain a complete social cross-section' (p. 15). Taylor tabulated the ability, based on tests of verbal reasoning, of children who, on an area basis, would have been admitted in 1964 to these 9 hypothetical schools. The scoring on this test took 100 or a little over as being the median of a child's verbal reasoning ability. Relatively few pupils scored over 130, or between 70 and 80. Nevertheless, in School B, only 85 pupils scored over 110, whilst in School D, 214 pupils made roughly equivalent scores. Taylor pointed out that in School D, of its eleven-form entry, four of those forms will be equivalent to grammar school entrants, and there will be only 12 children of below average ability. In contrast, School B 'has little more than a one-form grammar school entry combined with 83 Newsom children' (p. 15). (In the 1960s 'Newsom' was educationalese for below average ability children.) Taylor argued that: 'Two inevitable results of the maladministration of ability will be sixth forms varying widely in size and a concentration of well qualified staff in the schools known to have a large proportion of able children.' (p. 15.)

Taylor made a similar assessment assuming this time, somewhat more realistically, that the secondary schools would be five-, six- or seven-form entry (because of the necessity to use existing school buildings). This prognostication produced some interesting results: in part because of their greater realism. In School B1, there were 1 outstanding and 4 very able children, as compared with the 14 and 47 in school D2. Taylor wonders how these groups of able children will fare in the one school as opposed to the other. Taylor remarks: 'It would appear that parents selecting houses in the right areas have little to lose from comprehensive education; other parents of able children may be apprehensive.' (p. 16.)

Taylor's article turned out to be an accurate prediction of the difficulties facing LEAs in creating schools with a 'balanced' intake, or social mix. For instance, Professor Michael Rutter and his team of researchers, reported in *Fifteen Thousand Hours: Secondary Schools and their effects on children* on the educational progress of pupils at twelve schools in the Inner London Education Authority (ILEA) during the 1970s. Rutter comments: 'Despite administrative efforts to ensure that ability groupings should be reasonably comparable across all London schools, there were fairly major variations within our sample.' (1979, p. 154.) Only one school had pupils of whom one-quarter were deemed 'top ability'. In contrast, three of the twelve schools in the sample had less than 5 per cent of such children. There were similar differences in the occupational balance. Proportions of children from ethnic minorities varied most of all: from 4 per cent to 53 per cent. And this is in a system whereby the ILEA: 'aims both to meet parental wishes and to ensure a reasonable balance of children of all levels of abilities at each secondary school' (Rutter, p. 35).

Administrators and local politicians were urged to take the greatest care in drawing up catchment areas. Inevitably, this was a very difficult exercise, often conducted with a great deal of secrecy. Selection by ability and aptitude had been abandoned – to be replaced by selection by administrators and politicians. Many parents, of course, were not satisfied with the schools to which their children were allotted – in the same way that some parents had been dissatisfied by the results of the eleven-plus selection. In a few cases, appeal to the Ombudsman has been a moderately satisfactory way of redressing such grievances; if, that is, such misallocations revealed 'maladministration' on the part of the LEA. Other parents, rather than involving themselves in bureaucratic snarl-ups, placed their children in private schools, or simply moved house to a catchment area with a more favoured school. Thus owner-occupiers had something of an advantage over those in rented housing – particularly those within the council house system. The 1980 Education Act may make it easier for parents to select a comprehensive school of their choice – particularly as falling rolls have created space within schools: thus limiting ready use of the excuse 'no room at the school' as a means of enforcing a catchment area policy.

The difficulties facing politicians and administrators in creating comprehensive schools arise from the simple fact that the population is not randomly distributed. Rather, people are grouped, and group themselves, in ways that reflect differences of income and social status; and, to a lesser extent perhaps, religious affiliation and ethnic origin. In any large connurbation, residential areas can be clearly identified in terms of the level of income and occupational status of their inhabitants. Taylor, in the article referred to above, distinguished nine areas in north Leeds, all with differing characteristics; for example, area A ('A post-war housing estate together with an area of owner-occupied houses') contrasts with area E ('A very good residential area and a small post-war housing estate'), and so on.

Ironically enough, these differences (inequalities and therefore injustices in the eyes of some) have been exacerbated by the housing policies of national and local government. Such policies encouraged the building, particularly in the post-war years, of massive, municipally owned housing estates. This housing, built in many cases by local authorities dominated by the Labour Party, has been rented mainly by manual workers. Thus, a city such as Newcastle-upon-Tyne is divided into two types of housing: that owned by the local authorities; and that owner occupied. In a rough and ready way such divisions parallel differences in income and occupation.

There is evidence, in addition, that the housing policies of many local authorities actually refine these divisions. Whether intentionally or not, housing estates are finely graded until one comes to the 'sink' estate largely inhabited by families deemed to be problematic by the housing, probation, and social services departments. And, with rather the same consequences, speculative builders create housing estates attractive to different income groups. Writing in her political testament as a leading light of the newly created Social Democratic Party, Shirley Williams accurately observes: 'Housing has been segregated as well as education into council estates and private estates. Because most schools are neighbourhood schools, socially segregated housing becomes the foundation of socially segregated schools.' (*Politics is for People* 1981, p. 208.)

The reorganisation of secondary schooling in the cities and connurbations ran parallel with demographic, social and economic decline within them. Whilst the population of Britain has increased steadily this century, and the numbers living in our great connurbations has grown correspondingly, there have been important population shifts in the last couple of decades. Briefly, there has been a movement of population from the once crowded centres of Britain's cities to the outer suburbs and beyond. Those remaining behind included the elderly and those unable to move – perhaps lacking the necessary finance and job skills. There is a danger of exaggerating the poverty of social conditions in the inner-city areas. Not all their inhabitants are 'socially deprived' – to use a sociological cliché. Nevertheless inner-city areas have rather more than their proportionate share of unskilled workers, the unemployed, and of children from one-parent families, and from larger than average sized families.

These changes in the character of many of our big cities and connurbations, exacerbated the difficulties of educational administrators in creating comprehensive schools. In theory, all comprehensive schools are equal in their opportunities. In practice, as Professor Rutter's report suggests, in the centre of our big cities some schools are less equal than others. It may well be that such schools would have great difficulties even if secondary schools had not been reorganised. Nevertheless, some observations in *Aspects of Secondary Education in England: a Survey by HM Inspectors of Schools* are worth considering. In a comment on schools facing particular problems (many children with learning difficulties, social and psychological problems, etc.) comprehensive 're-organisation had made additional demands on frequently in-experienced and rapidly changing staff'. (1979, p. 255.) The Inspectorate noted: 'Within a few years, these schools had undergone changes in ability range, age range and size. Reorganisation in some schools had involved taking in children simultaneously at both 13-plus and 14-plus, and amalgamation of two or three very different schools and transfers from dissimilar institutions.' (p. 254.)

In addition, immigrants from the West Indies, from Bangladesh and from India, have sought to be housed in the inner-city areas, perhaps not always from choice. Immigrants have found housing in the inner-cities relatively cheap to buy or to rent. In contrast, residential rules and restrictions have sometimes limited the access of immigrants to council housing. Whatever their reason for their choice of housing, immigrants (and their children) are thus to be found in proportionately larger numbers in demarcated areas of British cities.

Such ethnic minority groups in British cities made visible the difficulties of creating schools that are 'socially and intellectually comprehensive' (as recommended by Circular 10/65). A handful of local authorities attempted to integrate their schools intellectually, and socially (and, therefore, racially) by a dispersal policy. This frequently involved bussing non-white children to schools which otherwise might have had a mainly white intake. Kirp, an American educationalist with a particular interest in matters of educational law and administration, contrasted British and

American policy (somewhat to the advantage of Britain) in his book intriguingly titled *Doing Good by Doing Little, Race and Schooling in Britain*. He instances Southall, in London, a number of whose non-white children were bussed to Ealing for the purpose of creating schools with something of a racial mix.

It is of interest that, as Kirp reports: 'large segments of Ealing's liberal and minority community came to regard dispersal as discriminatory'. By December 1974, the Ealing Borough Council agreed to abandon the policy of dispersal that had been followed since 1963. Kirp adds: 'Bussing, its opponents said, denied non-white parents choices available to whites.' (1979, p. 90.) Kirp, in a survey of attempts to disperse non-whites, concludes that dispersal as an explicit policy has been abandoned by local authorities. It is not acceptable to the white *or* the non-white communities. However, Kirp argues that where non-white children cannot be quietly and unobtrusively dispersed: 'the inevitable result is the emergence in minority-dominated neighbourhoods of what can only be termed ghetto schools, which provide an education equally as unsatisfactory as many American schools functioning in similar circumstances' (p. 102).

Community or comprehensive schooling?

I have argued in the above that going comprehensive runs counter to deep-seated social and economic trends. Secondary reorganisation was not, as its advocates claimed, a consequence of such movements. On the contrary, LEAs attempting to create comprehensive schools, ineffectively struggled against demographic, political, and social tendencies.

For this reason, it is understandably inconsistent of the supporters of comprehensive schooling to abandon the social case for comprehensive schools that Shirley Williams describes as unanswerable (1981, p. 156). For instance, Clyde Chitty, in a provocatively-entitled article, 'Why Comprehensive Schools?', condemned social mixing, perhaps with Shirley Williams in mind, as misbegotten Fabianism. Chitty informs us that in 1981 'It really does not matter whether or not a school is "socially comprehensive"; nor can it be expected to solve all the contradictions inherent in capitalist society.' (*Forum*, 1981, p. 5.) This is a conclusion presaged by Professor Brian Simon. Writing in the journal *Comprehensive Education*, he speculated: 'It may well be that this [comprehensive schooling] can best be achieved in a neighbourhood school – even when this is a "one-class" school –

which develops close links with the locality, parents, children and others, rather than in a school which takes in artificially, from outside its neighbourhood, a middle-class element in order to achieve social mixing.' (1966 p. 6.)

Some LEAs attempted to create neighbourhood or community schools somewhat along these lines in the 1970s. Two of the best known are Wyndham School in Egremont, Cumberland, and Countesthorpe College in Leicestershire. In this type of school there is an attempt to make available to all that live in the vicinity of the school the facilities it can provide. Thus, the school will not only be a place where, between nine and four o'clock, teachers teach and pupils learn; but it will, in addition, be open in the evening, weekends and during the holidays, for evening classes, drama groups, sporting activities, political meetings. Perhaps a part of the library will be open to general readers, or a coffee bar will be kept open to provide refreshment for those making use of the buildings, and their facilities in out-of-school hours. Such a school may encourage a wider interest in its activities by the general public by all manner of means. For example, teachers may be expected to make direct contact with parents and other adults interested in the work of the school.

Traditionally, schools in Britain have rather discouraged parents and the general public from taking too close an interest in their affairs. Parents have been kept in their proper place – at a distance – by any number of devices and stratagems: most of them familiar to those on both sides of the fence taking part in schools' open days and parents' evenings. Community schooling stops all that, and positively encourages parents to take part in school activities, and to join in the running and organising of the school. Parents in the 1970s became permitted, in their own right, to sit on the boards of governors that, at any rate in theory, control the maintained schools.[10] A community school is likely to encourage that trend by positively inviting parents, and other members of the local neighbourhood, to assist in the government of the school. Eric Midwinter, in the 1970s one of the most persuasive advocates of such schooling, characterised it in this way: 'As a theoretical goal we had defined the Community School as one which ventured out into and welcomed the comunity until a visionary time arrived when it was difficult to distinguish school from community.' (1972, p. 160.)

There may be much to be commended in the notion of the community school. Perhaps, regrettably, schools in Britain have ignored the neighbourhood in which they are to be found. Teachers, like the LEAs that employ them, may have an excessively paternalistic approach to the parents of the children they teach. They are, perhaps, only too ready to ignore the legitimate and rational demands of parents for information on the activities of the school; and too unwilling to consider the point of view of parents on matters of curriculum, school discipline, and organisation. Nevertheless, as Angela Skrimshire has pointed out, there is 'the danger of making the facilities and institutions available before the slow and difficult work of creating participation from the more "disadvantaged" groups has taken root. The structure may be taken over by the more affluent and articulate, and involvement by the disadvantaged thereby deterred' (In *Oxford Review of Education* 7 [1] 1981, p. 2).

However, the more fundamental question is: can a community school be comprehensive? In principle, this might be possible as a neighbourhood or community could, in a rough and ready way, be a microcosm of society. But, for reasons explored in the preceding section this is unlikely. The impression is that the advocates of comprehensive education, who want community schools, have abandoned (with Brian Simon and Eric Midwinter) the notion of a school that is 'socially and intellectually comprehensive'. Instead, they are advocating schools which specifically reflect the characteristics of the local community. In this way there would come into being (as a matter of deliberate policy rather than inadvertently) suburban schools and inner-city schools, rapidly to be labelled by the class conscious as middleclass and working-class schools respectively. It is not likely, either, that schools will be differentiated on class lines alone: for given that there are strong relationships between race and residence, some schools may become (again as a matter of policy) full of the children of ethnic minorities, whilst most will not.

Again, schools differentiated along lines of culture, class, and race, may be justified by some. In what way, however, can they be described as comprehensive schools? They do not satisfy the demand, made by many supporters of comprehensive schools in the 1960s, that such schools contain a 'social mix': the case for which was argued on social grounds; the case which Shirley Williams declares unanswerable.

Eric Midwinter, in addition, argued that such schools must be agents of 'community regeneration'. Schools will concentrate more of their time and energies on reviving and sustaining declining areas in our big cities. Such activities may take precedence over providing those sort of opportunities that typically take the brightest and the most energetic and enterprising of our boys and girls away from family and neighbourhood. One appreciates that there is a genuine loss to a local community if the ablest of its members depart to take their place in the larger community outside. Nevertheless, such neighbourhood schools need to think carefully before abandoning the provision of opportunities for occupational advancement equal to those of schools in the more privileged suburban localities. Community schooling may, indeed, be synonymous with a form of schooling intended to ensure that everyone keeps their place in society, and the abandonment of the principle of equality of opportunity. Yet another ground for believing that there is a contradiction in advocating both comprehensive *and* community schooling.

One cannot help suspecting that the great difficulties facing LEAs in creating schools which are 'socially and intellectually comprehensive' led to the abandonment of the belief, clearly expressed by Hinton that: 'a state school is more properly a microcosm of society rather than an extension of a sub-culture' (1979, p. 54). And yet it was on the basis of this – the social argument – that many people were persuaded of the desirability of comprehensive schooling.

Comprehensive or coexistence?

Creating neighbourhood schools – particularly in the inner areas of large cities – had the paradoxical consequence of permitting the independent, the voluntary schools, and some maintained grammar schools to flourish. Thus, in the early 1970s a number of LEAs, with the support of Margaret Thatcher, then Secretary of State for Education, adopted a policy of coexistence. In such LEAs, comprehensive schools were established on the lines of neighbourhood schools, whilst some grammar schools – particularly in the voluntary or denominational sector – were permitted to continue in existence. In particular, direct grant schools, in part financed by the DES, still continued to select up to half their pupils on the grounds of ability. The independent schools carried on much as before, but now very much aware of the political threat to their existence.

Indeed Mary Warnock argued for a policy of coexistence, seeing no difficulties arising for comprehensive schools from the existence of selection inside or outside the state system. Although a school is called 'comprehensive', 'It does not mean that no children can legitimately be educated in private schools or by tutors in their own home, or that a local authority is necessarily wrong to allow individual children to be educated in such schools.' (1979, p. 38.)

However, such a conclusion was vigorously denied by Caroline Benn in a pamphlet, written for the National Union of

Teachers and the Campaign for Comprehensive Education, and published in 1976 by the NUT. The pamphlet is entitled: '"We must choose which we want" a study of Coexistence and the problems of Incomplete Reorganization.' The quotation contained within the title comes from the Donnison Report (1970). This was the second report of the Public Schools Commission (PSC) and 'taken up with the issues of comprehensive education and their implications for a group of selective schools . . . [direct grant schools of]'quasi-independent status, with substantial numbers of fee-paying pupils' (Maclure, 1973, p. 343). The choice the Donnison Report starkly set before us was between the existence of any kind of selective school, fee-paying or otherwise, and comprehensive organisation ('Grammar schools of the traditional kind cannot be combined with a comprehensive system: we must choose which we want.' [Donnison Report, Vol. I, para. 259]).

The logic of comprehensive reorganisation, it appears, demands the abolition of *all* selective schooling. This is because the existence of selective schooling undermined the status and feasibility of the comprehensive schools. Caroline Benn provides in her pamphlet, a report of a survey of the effects of coexistence. This report suggests that coexistence lowered the number of high ability pupils in comprehensives, whilst correspondingly increasing the numbers of those with low ability. Benn states also that: 'Coexistence lowered the level of esteem the school had in the community.' (1976, p. 35.) Parents considered such a school to be a second-choice school. The numbers of middle-class children were limited, whilst there was a larger than proportionate number of problem children. Sixth forms were small in size. All these features of the schools had an inevitably deleterious influence on staff recruitment. Overall morale within such schools was low. Benn enunciated the 'law of coexistence': 'The selective school gets more selective, the comprehensives get less selective. That is the law of coexistence.' (1976, p. 41).

Parents favoured the grammar school to the neighbourhood comprehensive. Benn quotes the head of an ex-secondary modern school as saying: 'The comprehensive principle . . . is weakened . . . by the massive use of parental option to the . . . old grammar school. We lose up to 20 per cent of the middle-class pupils of the area to the comprehensive based on the old grammar (school). The comprehensive system is honoured in the letter, but destroyed by the abuse of parental option.' (p. 27).

The evils of coexistence then demand not only the abolition of all schooling other than the state-provided comprehensive school, but also the elimination of 'the abuse of parental option'.

This latter necessity is strongly argued for in a contribution to the journal, *Comprehensive Education,* by Barbara Bullivant, one-time national secretary of the pressure group, Campaign for the Advancement of State Education. Bullivant sees: 'grave dangers in unrestricted right of choice' (1978, p. 22). One such danger is that parental choices 'may operate against a particular school, in favour of a particular school . . .'. Other dangers arise from the ignorance of parents (who need 'education about education' (p. 22)); and the non-educational, and therefore wrong-headed, reasons parents may hold for preferring one school to another for their child. However, parental ignorance of comprehensive schools may not be mended by the publication of exam results, for this 'may lead to comparisons' in which some schools may be considered better than others.

Bullivant, it is clear, is strongly opposed to parents having even the limited right to choose a school for their children under current legislation. Indeed: 'Some parents might dislike the way some schools are organised' for (to Bullivant) the wholly irrelevant and non-educational reason that 'the school is too rough' for their child. She is sharply aware that freedom to choose a school will subvert the comprehensive system, for: 'if it is parental choice which decides allocation to a school, is this not even less fair than the old eleven-plus system, with "snob" schools for those whose parents know how to choose, and "sink" schools for those whose parents don't know, or don't care' (p. 23). Selection and choice by parents must be replaced with allocation by educational officials and local politicians, with their more complete (and secret) educational expertise; officials and politicians who have, in addition, the capacity to distinguish between the educational and the non-educational in their decision-making.

By the mid-1970s, Caroline Benn ruefully noted that, what for her was the slow pace of comprehensive reorganisation, had: 'resulted in a new bipartite system which in many ways is more polarised than when the country was officially bipartite' (1976, p. 1). In other words, comprehensive reorganisation to that date had increased educational and social inequalities. As ever things were getting worse before they could possibly become better. What was therefore necessary according to Benn, speaking for the comprehensive school lobby, was yet more comprehensive reorganisation, not less. In order to make such comprehensive reorganisation mandatory on those few LEAs, who had held out against the blandishments and the bullying of central government to go comprehensive, the 1976 Education Act was passed. From henceforward, at least for state schools, 'education is to be provided only in schools where the arrangements for the admission of pupils are not based (wholly, or partly) on selection by ability or aptitude' (s.1., 'The comprehensive principle').

The abolition of independent schooling

Given that the politics of education were largely in the hands of the supporters of comprehensive reorganisation, the abolition of maintained grammar schools was a relatively easy task to accomplish in the mid-70s; and was enforced in law by the 1976 Education Act. As Fenwick observes: 'Under a committed national government, groups opposed to comprehensive reorganisation were restricted to fighting procedure for planning and implementing change.' (1976, p. 163.) The way in which the independent schools remained to fulfil Caroline Benn's Law of Coexistence ('The selective school gets more selective, the comprehensives get less selective') became ever more visible.

Why are the independent schools seen as so much of a threat to the comprehensive system? After all, only a tiny minority of children attend such schools; estimates vary, but probably no more than about 5 per cent (see chapter 1). In addition, parents pay fees for their children to be taught at such schools, and are not taxed or rated less for not making use of state schools. Thus they relieve the state system of the costs of paying for their children whilst not foregoing the payment of taxes and rates which go, in part, to pay for the education of children in the maintained schools.

At least three reasons may be adduced from the writings of the comprehensive school lobby. The first is that such schools 'cream' some of the ablest (and middle-class) children away from comprehensive system – thus making it less truly comprehensive. Independent schools illustrate Benn's Law of Coexistence in action. The Donnison Report (1970) put this point well: 'It follows from our principles for [comprehensive] reorganisation that there can, ultimately, be no place for fee-paying in schools coming wholly in a comprehensive system. . . . Here we need only point out that to permit the payments of fees to play any part in selection would clearly threaten the aims of reorganisation . . .' (quoted in Maclure, 1973, p. 350).

In the second place, independent schools are, from the point of view of the comprehensive school lobby, indefensible bastions of privilege that have no place in a democratic and socialist society. Daunt, for instance, calls for the 'total elimination of the independent schools, because they far more than any other single institution or custom, perpetuate the "hoary social curse" of the uniquely divisive and persistent English and Scottish class systems, which falsify humanity and debilitate society' (1975, p. 20). Indeed, the Public Schools Commission, in their first publication, the Newsom Report (1968), condemned the public schools (defined as those independent schools at the time in the membership of the Headmasters' Conference, Governing Bodies Association, or Governing Bodies of Girls' Schools Association) as being socially divisive. Newsom claimed that such schools were exclusive and inhabited a world of their own. In addition, such schools confer educational opportunities and advantages 'on an arbitrarily selected membership, which already starts with an advantageous position in life' (quoted in Maclure, 1973, p. 338). Thus the independent schools (or at least the public schools) were accused of maintaining, if not creating, those social divisions of one kind or another that were wholly repugnant to the membership of the Public Schools Commission.

It is noteworthy that the terms of reference of the Commission included the instruction that it investigate how best 'To create a socially mixed entry into the [public] schools in order . . . to reduce the divisive influence which they now exert.' (quoted in Maclure, 1973, p. 333.) The notion that the causes of social divisions (putting on one side their alleged undesirability) might not be found within schools, private or state, seems never to have crossed the minds of the Commission. Perhaps it should have asked whether societies without the detested private schooling (such as the USSR) are any less socially divided than our own allegedly class-ridden country. The results of such an enquiry might have dented their simple faith that it is schools, rather than societies, that exert a 'divisive influence'.

The third reason for abolishing private schooling, as demanded by many supporters of comprehensive reorganisation, is that such schools are independent of the state, and, as such, not subject to 'democratic' control and surveillance. Hugh Gaitskell tried and failed, in the 1950s, to remove from the Labour Party constitution its clause four: that demands public and, therefore, state ownership of: 'all the means of production, distribution and exchange'. As Antony Flew points out, the clause 'presumably embraces the production, distribution and exchange of health, education, and welfare services as well as – what shall we say? – corporeal goods' (1981, p. 12). And, in so far as comprehensive schooling is, in John White's words already quoted, 'an integral part of the socialist vision', it is incompatable with the notion of any schooling free of state control.

A comprehensive system of education, then, demands (contrary to Mary Warnock's optimistic reasoning) the elimination of private and independent schools. This point is strongly made by Daunt, in his book *Comprehensive Values* published after he had resigned his comprehensive school headship to become a member of the Education Directorate of the EEC. Daunt states as his *credo*: 'I believe that there is *nothing more important* for education in Britain – not even the completion of comprehensive reorganisation within the state system let alone the abolition of public examinations at sixteen . . . than the *total abolition* of the independent schools . . .' (my italics 1975, p. 103).

A number of years earlier, the Labour politician, C. A. R. Crosland seems to have come to a rather similar conclusion: 'It would . . . be absurd from a socialist point of view to close down the grammar schools, while leaving the public schools still holding their present commanding position.' (1956, p. 275.) But, unlike many socialists and educationalists, he considered how best ('from a socialist point of view') to bring such schools down from 'their present commanding position'. He rejected total abolition – no doubt with regret – with the argument that: 'It is out of tune with the temper of the country, and is therefore not likely in any event to be politically practicable.' (p. 262.) And, if the findings of a NOP poll, commissioned by *The Observer* and published therein, are to be relied upon, abolition still remains 'out of tune with the temper of the country'. (8 February 1981.) (Although whether such a fact renders any future policy of total abolition by some future Labour government 'not politically practicable' may now be doubted.)

The NOP poll revealed that most of its respondents opposed abolition. In addition, 72 per cent of respondents, if money was no problem, would choose an independent fee-paying school for their children if they were unable to get the state school of their choice. And when parents, who had chosen a state school for children, were asked what had influenced their decision, very nearly 70 per cent of them gave as the major reason for their choice: 'It costs too much to send a child to a fee-paying school.' Indeed there is remarkable consistency in the findings of pollsters on attitudes to independent schooling. The Research Services poll commissioned by *New Society*, found over 70 per cent of its respondents in favour of retaining independent schooling, and only 18 per cent against (see *New Society*, 26 October 1967). Ten years earlier in 1957, a poll commissioned by the Labour Party found only 8 per cent willing to abolish public schools, whilst 52 per cent wanted to leave them unaltered. 80 per cent of parents were prepared to pay for education privately; and only 23 per cent of Labour Party supporters opposed such expenditure on ideological grounds. It is partly in the light of findings of this kind that Labour politicians have so far drawn back from the outright abolition of independent and private schooling.

Most recently *The Sunday Times* published some details of polls conducted on the popularity of independent and private schools. In an article 'Why parents choose private schools,' it was stated: 'Among the leaders and opinion-formers of British society, there is an overwhelming vote for independent education' (28 February 1982, p. 13). This generalisation was based upon a postal survey which culled 600 replies from MPs, top civil servants, company directors, Oxbridge dons, QCs, comprehensive head-teachers, and others. Of these 600 top people, 322 paid school fees for at least one of their children. Whether this is evidence of 'an overwhelming vote for independent education' might be doubted – but it was at least a straw in the wind. Perhaps even more of interest than the expected conclusion that top people send their children to independent schools, was the revelation that 'a significant minority of comprehensive heads send their own children to private schools'.[11]

Crosland was also aware that 'flat proscription is undesirable on libertarian grounds' (1956, p. 262). If abolition is therefore both unpopular and unethical: what is to be done? Crosland seized upon the notion of 'integration' as the socialist – but democratic and libertarian – solution to the problem of what to do about the independent schools. He argued that 'the most sensible approach is to work for a gradual integration of these schools into the State system of education' (1956, p. 263). 'Integration' certainly has a happier sound about it than abolition, or elimination, but are these notions to be distinguished? If independent schools are integrated in the state system of education, in what way will such schools remain independent, private and fee paying? Their existence will be akin to the smile of the Cheshire cat after its bodily disappearance. ('Well! I've often seen a cat without a grin,' thought Alice; 'but a grin without a cat! It's the most curious thing I ever saw in all my life!') As Brenda Cohen remarks in *Education and the Individual,* 'in effect and in outcome it is impossible to distinguish the objective of full integration from that of abolition. The distinction between the two aims is purely semantic' (1981, p. 18).

However, Crosland as a practical politician was not to be deterred from employing a distinction without a difference. In 1965, Crosland, now Secretary of State for Education, set up the Public Schools Commission (PSC) and gave it the brief: 'To recommend a national plan for integrating the schools with the maintained sector of education.' (quoted in Maclure, 1973, p. 332.) Such a brief was tantamount to instructing a doctor to kill his patient whilst keeping him alive. In the words of Dr John Rae, headmaster of Westminster School, writing in *The Public School Revolution* (1981): 'Like the victim of an epidemic, the Commission's First Report was buried quickly and without ceremony.' In 1971, and now out of office, Crosland remarked that his civil servants at the DES: 'were sceptical as to whether the government knew what it was doing [in setting up the PSC]. They rightly challenged me on whether there was any possible compromise solution which a commission could recommend and which stood a chance of acceptance on both financial and political grounds' (in conversation with Professor Kogan, 1971, p. 177). Crosland, in that same conversation, confessed: 'I must say that much of their scepticism eventually proved justified.'

The direct grant schools turned out to be an easier target. The Public Schools Commission was reconstituted in 1968, and Professor David Donnison (described by John Rae as 'that familiar English figure, the ex-public school boy who was determined to reform the public schools' (1981, p. 39)), replaced Sir John Newsom as chairman. In 1967 the terms of reference had been increased 'To advise on the most effective method or methods by which direct grant grammar schools . . . can participate in the movement towards comprehensive reorganisation.' (Maclure, 1973, p. 337). The Donnison Report came to the wholly predictable conclusion that the elimination of direct grant grammar schools was the most effective method by which such schools could 'participate in the movement towards comprehensive reorganisation'. Or to put it another way, Scheme A in the report (supported by seven members) recommended the schools to continue to be funded from central government, but to become non-selective, and to be reorganised along lines broadly similar to those set out in section 1 of Circular 10/65. Another seven members urged that the direct grant schools become LEA controlled or aided schools (Scheme B). The chairman, Professor Donnison, was happy with either scheme, as both amounted to more or less the same thing: the abolition of the direct grant schools.

The direct grant schools were a curious and interesting anomaly in the British educational system. They occupied a place halfway between the independent and the maintained schools. In part, direct grant schools were financed directly by the DES (hence their name); in part by LEAs paying fees for the 25–50 per cent of free and reserved places such schools were obliged to allocate to the LEAs; and, in part, by fees from parents for the residuary places. In addition, such schools raised money by appeals, endowments, etc., as do the independent schools. Direct grant schools varied considerably in size and general characteristics: some were denominational and single sex; and some were members of those bodies (like the HMC) that confer the cachet of 'public school'. The best of them had an enviable academic reputation (it is perhaps invidious to pick out any one, but all readers will know of the Manchester Grammar School) and were more successful than all other types of schools in gaining scholarships to Oxford and Cambridge colleges.

In addition, some claim can be made that they were truly comprehensive schools – at least in terms of a fair spread of ability and social background. In part, this was a consequence of their substantial entry from LEAs; and, whilst the LEA entry was by selection and competition, Saran (1973, p. 190) notes that: 'only 31 per cent of residuary place entrants [fee-paying] had been graded by their LEA as suitable for a grammar school education.' Nevertheless, despite or because of all these estimable features, the Donnison Report argued: 'In some areas it will be impossible to carry through comprehensive reorganisation . . . if the direct grant schools continue their present role' (1970, para. 222). In 1975, the Labour government decided to stop funding such schools, and out of the 178 schools of direct grant list 119 chose to go independent rather than be integrated or absorbed into the state system.

Thus far we have reached an impasse. Most children in Britain are now in some kind or other of comprehensive school. A minority are taught in independent or private schools. Indeed, paradoxically, such schooling has been sustained by comprehensive reorganisation. It had been the hope and earnest wish of socialists, such as R. H. Tawney, that the state system of education would become so attractive to parents and children that independent schooling would wither away from lack of support. Crosland, to the indignation of some of his socialist colleagues, wrote in *The Future of Socialism* of independent schools: 'That these schools are superior, and notably the "public schools", is beyond dispute.' (1956, p. 261.) In 1983, this opinion may be more widely shared than in 1956; and as Dr Rae points out, and writing as a head of a popular independent day school: 'parents were willing to pay the ever-increasing fees for private schools because they were dissatisfied with the education the maintained schools had to offer' (1981, p. 176).

5 The organisation of comprehensive schools: one

'The object of having comprehensive schools is not to
abolish all competition and all envy, which might be rather a
hopeless task, but to avoid the extreme social division
caused by physical segregation into schools of widely
divergent status, and the extreme social resentment caused
by failure to win a grammar (or, in future, public) school
place, when this is thought to be the only avenue to a
"middle-class" occupation.' C. A. R. Crosland, 1956.

A question of size?

In the last two chapters I have outlined the ways in which the
school system was reformed along comprehensive lines. I have
argued that such a reorganisation had little popular support
either with parents or teachers. It was brought about by the
calculated use of political power at local and national level. Nor is
there much evidence that the reforms have created comprehensive schools along the lines envisaged in Circular 10/65. Comprehensive reorganisation has created a network of neighbourhood
schools whose features are largely dependent upon the character
of the neighbourhoods in which they are to be found. The lack of
any national plan has resulted, as noted by Benn and Simon, in
local schemes of reorganisation that are 'bewilderingly various
from area to area' (1970, p. 43). The notion of the comprehensive
school as a microcosm of society has been well-nigh impossible to
fulfil in practice.

If the reorganisation of the secondary *system* of education has
failed, what of the organisation of the schools themselves?
Supporters of secondary-school reform, on the whole, believed
that the reorganisation of the system of education was but a
beginning in the more fundamental task of the reform of edu-

cation seen in its entirety. There was surely no point, for example, in abolishing selection by ability between schools if such selection were to reappear within them. Brian Simon and Caroline Benn make this quite clear as when, in their report on the then progress toward comprehensive reorganisation, they assert: 'The practice of strict streaming . . . is a practice clearly incompatible with genuine comprehensive reorganisation in the long run.' *Half Way There* (1971, p. 360.) And more recently, Caroline Benn, as spokesperson for the pressure group entitled 'Right to a Comprehensive Education', and in a letter to *The Times Educational Supplement* (25 September, 1981), claimed and deplored, that 'selection still takes place inside individual comprehensive schools themselves'.

It must be said, however, that not quite all the advocates of comprehensive reorganisation recommended a radical re-shaping of the schools created by such a reform. Outstanding amongst the supporters of such reorganisation was C. A. R. Crosland. As the politician responsible for Circular 10/65, he helped to get the bandwagon rolling. Crosland argued in 1956 that 'The object of having comprehensive schools is not to abolish all competition and all envy . . .'. Even a socialist politician could recognise this as 'rather a hopeless task'. The point of it all is: 'to avoid the extreme social division caused by physical segregation into schools of widely divergent status' (Crosland, 1956, p. 272). Whether this has been the consequence of comprehensive reorganisation I have been at pains to doubt. Crosland was also eager to eliminate the possibility of 'the extreme social resentment caused by failure to win a grammar (or, in future, public) school place, when this is thought to be the only avenue to a "middle-class" occupation' (p. 272). Again we may remain sceptical that such a vaguely described 'social resentment' may be eliminated by the abolition of grammar and public schools. Nevertheless, the reorganisation of schools was to be limited to the abolition of selection for entry by ability and aptitude; for *within* the comprehensive school Crosland argued: 'Division into streams according to ability remains essential.' (1956, p. 272.)

Crosland may have found, like many, however, that reforms have a habit of running away with the would-be reformer. Few of the supporters of comprehensive school reorganisation were happy to see such a reform as having as its limited aim the avoidance of 'the extreme social division caused by physical segregation into schools of widely divergent status' (see Crosland above). And whilst envy of those successful in gaining entry to grammar schools could be encouraged in the interests of destroying the selective system, comprehensive school reformers such as

P. E. Daunt, were seeking to reduce the influence of the school in promoting any kind of occupational success – particularly to 'middle-class' jobs. For schools, in attempting to satisfy the occupational aspiration of their pupils, were in danger of creating that meritocratic society many comprehensive school reformers wished to destroy. Indeed, Daunt described the new 'way of valuing people and activities' within the comprehensive school as a kind of 'Copernican revolution'. Such a revolution meant that the comprehensive school 'is asking the public to esteem it in an entirely new way.' (Daunt, 1975, p. 101.)

The avowed principles underpinning this revolution may be characterised (with a nod to the rather more famous ideals of the French Revolution) as: 'Equality, Opportunity, Community'. The comprehensive school was to provide opportunities open to and equal for all, within a school community which itself was an indissoluble part of the local community without. At Wyndham School in Cumbria, its headmaster, John Sharp, recounts how these ideals were expressed on a tablet of stone decorating the school's central block. This stone dedicated the school to 'the brotherhood of man . . . to the open mind and to the open door' (1973, p. 6). There was further provided a list of names of those who were presumably thought best to exemplify the brotherhood of man: Gandhi; Albert Schweitzer; Luther King; Bertrand Russell; John Kennedy; Albert Luthuli; Pope John XXIII. . . . Sharp records that the list of about twenty names is steadily growing. But how, apart from their rendering in stone, the ideals of the comprehensive school could be achieved in practice remained a matter of controversy. No more so than over the size of the schools; for what is the ideal size of the comprehensive school?

In the selective system, schools had been quite small: 300 pupils were normal for a secondary modern, and a grammar school may have been typically a little larger with about 400 pupils in all. In schools of such a size their organisation could be relatively simple and uncomplicated. However, that was all to change with the arrival of the comprehensive school.

Indeed, in the immediate post-war years, the projected size of a comprehensive school was seen by its opponents as an irrefutable argument against it.[12] The notion of a school of 2,000 pupils was thought to be impractical and unspeakable, contrary to all the traditions within British schooling. The size of the putative comprehensive school was calculated, employing two important assumptions. The first was that such a school would be provided for all children between the ages of eleven and eighteen; and second, that, relatively speaking, only a small proportion of pupils would stay on after the then school-leaving age of fifteen, either to complete five-year GCE 'O' level courses, or to proceed into the sixth form, that, in turn, was seen as providing GCE 'A' level courses largely for those pupils going on to higher education.

Indeed, such were the assumptions of Circular 10/65. The 'orthodox comprehensive school' for pupils aged between eleven to eighteen was seen therein as providing 'in many respects the simplest and best solution' (para 6). However, optimism that the rate of stopping on after the compulsory school-leaving age would continue to increase, along with the determination to raise that age, modified the advice on school size. Circular 10/65 claimed then: 'It is now clear that a six- or seven-form entry school can cater properly for the whole ability range and produce a viable sixth form.' (para. 7.) The reference here to 'the whole ability range' is a reminder that if, in Robin Pedley's words the comprehensive school is to be 'justified principally by the accepted need to give maximum opportunity for self-fulfilment to each and all' (1978, p. 99), then staffing and facilities must be sufficient for that greater range of ability.

At one end of the ability range there will be required teachers for those most able academically; whilst at the other, teachers skilled in remedying a variety of educational disabilities. Whilst a grammar school might somewhat neglect instruction in the practical arts and crafts in the belief that 'the grammar school, whatever its variations, is essentially for those who can learn from books' (Davis, 1967), this is not a path to be followed by a comprehensive school. Nor can a comprehensive so neglect the world of books as to be without a library of any sort, and as in a secondary modern school described in the Newsom Report, keep its class and subject libraries 'in portable infant type cupboards' (1963, para. 58). Given then, the demand for a wide curriculum, and the staffing and facilities thus required, a six- or seven-form entry school might still be considered on the small size to 'give the maximum opportunity for self-fulfilment to each and all'. As headmaster Michael Hinton remarks, 'It is impossible to provide this variety with present staffing ratios unless the school takes at least six forms of entry, and preferably eight or nine.' (1979, p. 68.) And even a sixth-form entry (given 30 pupils per form for five years, plus 140 pupils as the DES recommended minimum size for an adequate sixth form) creates a school of 1040 pupils – more than twice the size of schools within the former selective system. Nor is there much indication that economies of scale are a consequence of this growth in size: for a larger school demands more administration and organisation which, in turn, necessitates an increase in secretarial and administrative staff. In addition, some staff are recruited only partly to teach, and rather more to guide and counsel this greater press of young people within the school.

And yet, despite the fact the logic of comprehensive schooling demands that its schools be large, this is a consequence un-welcome to the supporters of such schools – and most strongly disturbing to those whose task it is to organise, administer and control them. For example, Peter Dawson, headmaster from 1971 to 1980 of Eltham Green School, in his aptly entitled book, *Making a Comprehensive Work*, points out that: 'Anyone who denies that the large school generates problems of its own by its very size is blind to the obvious.' (1981 p. 2.) And no doubt with his own experience in leading his school along, in the words of the sub-title of his book, 'the road from bomb alley', Dawson adds: 'This is especially true when the monster is out of control.' (p. 2.)

Elizabeth Halsall provides an illustration of the practical dif-ficulties of control caused by size alone. In a large school with the fourth- and fifth-year pupils following a complex variety of subject options (as is the pattern in many schools), 'they [the pupils] may be arriving at a particular classroom from as many as half a dozen or more other classrooms, of which at least one is likely to be on the other side of the campus'. With the inevitable and predictable consequence: 'Since no lesson starts until every pupil, or almost every pupil has arrived, on each of these occasions there will be maximum delay and the *bigger the school* the greater the delay.' (Halsall, 1972, p. 96, my italics.)

In addition, large schools make it more difficult to approach the ideals of community and fraternity. John Watts, principal of the controversy-creating Countesthorpe College from 1972, points out that 'Nobody can *care* in any true sense of the word for 1,000 others: you can hardly know their names.' (1980, p. 167.) This fact has consequences for general supervision of children, for, as Halsall observes, where the teacher 'is not too sure of a child's name, has too far to walk, or knows he has not much chance of finding a relevant member of staff, he is less likely to take action' (1972, p. 99). Small schools, according to Robin Pedley, provide children with more opportunities to feel important than do the larger schools. Indeed Pedley, for all that he advocates compre-hensive reform leading to the establishment of large schools, quotes research evidence suggesting that in small schools, rather than in larger, pupils 'participate more fully and intensively in the activities provided and in more of them – an experience which incidentally makes them more versatile, but whose main justifi-cation is the satisfaction and confidence which they gain there-from' (1978, p. 78).

It is one of the paradoxes of comprehensive education that

although it is difficult to provide a full range of courses for a general spread of ability (putting on one side the very great difficulties in creating such schools in practice) without creating a large school of 1,000 pupils or more, nevertheless size in itself may not place such opportunities within every pupil's grasp. As former headmaster Maurice Holt observes: 'the inherent advantages of the large school, in terms of choice of subject and courses, are not in practice so easy to realise because of logistic problems arising from timetabling, staffing and accommodation' (1978, p. 17). A large school with a complicated option scheme for the fourth and fifth year, with pupils preparing for a variety of examinations, CSE, GCE 'O' and 'A' levels, requires a carefully plotted and prepared timetable to work at all. The danger is that the timetable begins to run the school, permitting little in the way of flexibility and limiting as many opportunities to pursue courses as it creates. John Sharp indeed laments that 'once the timetable has been drawn up, it is almost unthinkable to make any major changes for the year, simply because so much other change would be involved' (1973, p. 106).

In practice, comprehensive schools in England vary considerably in size. This fact should by now come as no surprise given the haphazard and unsystematic way in which the country has gone comprehensive. So varied is the pattern of the comprehensive reorganisation that the statisticians at the DES have devised 18 or more separate categories by which to organise statistical data on the pupil size and number of comprehensive schools. In January 1979, there were 1,470 11–18 'all-through' schools in England. Their sizes varied from 800 to over 2,000; indeed 13 schools had at that time over 2,000 pupils. The second largest category of secondary schools in England is for pupils aged eleven to sixteen; there were 821 in this group in 1979, with a considerable range of size from somewhat over 200 to well over 1,000 pupils in size. There were 9 11–16 schools which had between 1,500 to 2,000 pupils.

However, the fragmentation of the secondary school has had an inevitable influence on its size. In 1979, in LEAs operating a middle-school system, excluding both 'middle schools deemed primary' and sixth-form colleges within the system, there were seven separate categories of schools. One example of variation in size is found within the group of 256 schools catering for pupils between thirteen and eighteen. In this category there were 8 schools of less than 400 pupils at one extreme, and 4 schools with 2,000 pupils each at the other.

A rather similarly varied pattern can be seen in the 8 categories employed to provide information on the two-tier systems, whereby children enter a junior secondary school at eleven, but may or must leave at thirteen or fourteen to enter senior schools operating (at least in 1979) automatic or optional transfer systems. Many of these schools are relatively small, but the two-tier system has organisational disadvantages, so clearly forecast in Circular 10/65, 'particularly when a senior school is fed by more than one junior school' (para. 10, and see chapter 4).

One wonders at the state of British schooling in view of such a variety of organisation and size. How can schools for children between eleven and sixteen provide an adequate comprehensive curriculum – given present staffing ratios – if they contain less than 400 pupils – as did at least 46 such schools in 1979? It may be suspected that, in a number of cases, their ability range was as limited – indeed (who knows?) perhaps more so – as that of the secondary moderns, comprehensive schooling is alleged to have replaced. There are at the other extreme a number of schools with over 1,000 pupils – indeed, as noted, 13 all-through schools had over 2,000 pupils. And yet, comprehensive school supporters have shown considerable doubts about the virtues of size: for them, bigger is not necessarily better.

One further practical difficulty facing large schools is truancy. There is some evidence that in big cities school attendance – at least at the secondary stage – has become mainly voluntary. Large schools may have helped to bring about this state of affairs. Such schools often draw their pupils from an extensive and irregularly shaped catchment area. In circumstances when pupils have, perforce, to rely on public transport to get to school, any failure or irregularities of such a service provide a ready excuse and reason for non-attendance. And, however devoted teachers are to the mundane every-day task of registering pupils, the very complexity of organisation in the large school may make it all that more difficult for teachers to discover if pupils are indeed attending classes after registration. The scattered buildings of the comprehensive school – often on more than one site – provide opportunities galore for the truant to escape undetected. Some comprehensive school supporters consider the 'openness' of these schools a chief virtue. However, this very openness does make attendance at them more voluntary than compulsory, in contravention of law and the intentions of well-meaning educational reformers.

Falling rolls and shrinking schools

The school population in England and Wales rose between 1946 and 1976 from five to nine millions. Thus the secondary school system was reorganised at a time when the numbers of pupils in school were increasing. This was greatly to the advantage of the reformers. The increase in school numbers demanded more money for education: resources that were used, in part, to create 'purpose-built' comprehensives, but more generally to extend and alter old buildings. Undoubtedly, the greater numbers in schools helped to cushion the impact of comprehensive reform. In an expanding school system teachers could easily find jobs – or be found them by local authorities eager to limit teacher opposition to their schemes of reorganisation. Promotion in the late 1960s and early 1970s was relatively easy and open to many teachers. All this helped to reduce the possibility of a rebellion of teachers against the reorganisation of secondary schools.

The growth of the school population also enabled the LEAs to create the large schools, obviously necessary for even the most half-hearted forms of comprehensive reorganisation. Throughout the 1960s and early 1970s, resources for schools were scarce relative to demand. Teachers could pick and choose their jobs. They could leave after completing a term's teaching at one school and find another appointment in a neighbouring or distant LEA with little difficulty. Schools and authorities were grateful for all and any staff that came their way. Sometimes LEAs showed an understandable reluctance to enquire very deeply as to the suitability of their teachers for posts to which they were eagerly appointed. This was particularly the case with authorities least popular with teachers – those with schools in the central areas of large cities, or in the local authority housing estates built in the 1960s. In these areas, LEAs had to offer special inducements (greater allowances, help with accommodation, etc.) to staff their schools at all. During this period, teachers were a rationed commodity; LEAs could recruit only up to nationally agreed quotas.

Possibly the only losers in all this were pupils and their parents. A number of official reports, such as Newsom (1963), pointed to the facts of inadequate secondary school building with limited accommodation for practical and scientific activities, poor library space, etc. In addition, such reports described the instability of staffing in many schools, with staff remaining in post for a brief period before moving on. What a contrast to the stereotype of the teacher as an 'Old Mr Chips', reluctant to leave, out of a fierce loyalty to his school and a keen sense of professional responsibility to his pupils. The creation of comprehensive schools did nothing to stop this whirligig; rather the contrary, as reorganisation necessitated the reshaping of the school system, and the organisation of the schools into larger and larger units.

Schools, teachers, and the LEAs were in a seller's market. Their services were limited relative to the demand for them. Parents could not then pick and choose – unless they were prepared (and had sufficient means) to educate their children outside the state system. When schools were overcrowded, with lessons taught in all kinds of temporary accommodation, and with some schools not quite sure from one academic year to the next whether they would be properly staffed, parents might be grateful to have their children in any school perceived to be moderately satisfactory. From about the mid-1970s this position began to change.

Whilst in 1972 DES projections of the future school population assumed continued growth, by 1974 those same projections had been considerably revised with a substantial drop in pupil numbers predicted. How substantial this drop is may be gauged by the observation of Professor Eric Briault, formerly Chief Education Officer of ILEA, and writing in *Falling Rolls in Secondary Schools*: 'On any showing, the total secondary school numbers in 1991 will be less than three-quarters of the 1979 provisional numbers and, on the DES "principal projection", only a little above this in 1996' (1980, p. 20).

What is, and will be, the effect of falling numbers upon comprehensive schools and the system within which they are placed? First, falling rolls in schools sharpen the dilemma of parental choice. As school numbers decline, there is created more space within the schools themselves. Local authorities can no longer so easily turn away children from a popular school on the grounds of overcrowding. Professor Briault considers that parental choice is 'a major policy issue facing LEAs as rolls fall' (1980, p. 52). Briault claims: 'The issue may be simply stated: are parents to choose the schools they prefer or is contraction to be planned, controlled and managed at the expense of parents' freedom of choice?' (p. 520.)

Prescient supporters of secondary reorganisation had not overlooked the dangers to the comprehensive system of permitting 'parents to choose the school they prefer'. I have already noted (chapter 4) Barbara Bullivant's rhetorical question about allowing parental choice: 'is this not even less fair than the old eleven-plus system, with "snob" schools for those whose parents know how to choose, and "sink" schools for those whose parents don't know, or don't care? (1977/78, p. 23.) Caroline Benn is, however, prepared to countenance LEAs giving 'parents as much of a "say" as possible . . . so long as this is consistent with the principle of maintaining a comprehensive system and so long as all parents' preferences get equal attention' (1976, p. 3). Dr W. F. Dennison, a senior lecturer in education at Newcastle-upon-Tyne

University, puts Bullivant's point somewhat more soberly in these words: '. . . parental freedom can easily promote segregation. At one extreme, there will be schools where many parents have taken a positive decision to send their children. . . . At the other extreme there will be schools where the majority choice is effectively a process of non-selection by unconcerned parents.' (p. 66.) Indeed Dennison, in his study of the possible implications for schools of falling rolls, *Education in Jeopardy: Problems and Possibilities of Contraction*, believes that 'some of the adverse effects of parental choice have become evident in large cities' (1981, p. 66). And amongst those 'adverse effects' is the possibility of maintaining comprehensive schools in anything but name.

It appears, then, that the comprehensive system may only be maintained by denying, or at least severely limiting, any opportunity for parents to choose a school for their child. And yet the law permits a certain measure of parental choice. It may be disputed whether the 1980 Education Act has genuinely extended the freedom of parents to choose. Nevertheless, the 1980 Education Act does lay it as a duty upon LEAs both to enquire as to the school preferences of parents and 'to comply, except in certain cases, with this preference' (Taylor and Saunders, 1980, p. A8). This duty is, of course, hedged about; for example it does not apply 'if compliance with the preference would prejudice the provision of efficient education or the efficient use of resources' (1980 Education Act, S. 6 (3)(a)). However, the promise is there, and LEAs will have some fewer excuses for denying the reasonable exercise of parental choice. Dennison asks plaintively (and no wonder), 'Could it be that, in circumstances of pupil decline, consumer choice and administrative control are incompatible, and that the dilemmas of the administrator are insoluble?' (1981, p. 75.)

Secondly, falling rolls have (and shall) lead to school closures. This is politically unpopular even with schools that are relatively undersubscribed. The general tendency of such closure will be to concentrate children into somewhat fewer, but somewhat larger schools. Small schools will be the ones most at risk as the school system contracts. On the one hand, small secondary schools (now often defined as those with less than 700 pupils), it will be claimed, cannot offer a curriculum broad enough for a *comprehensive* school. And, on the other hand, it has become imperative for LEAs to fill their largest schools as best they can – in order to keep them open at all in the light of the very considerable costs of heating, cleaning, and maintaining the largest of our schools. These large schools may only be retained at the cost of closing smaller schools, whose closure may, in any case, be somewhat easier from a political and administrative outlook. No doubt a system of large comprehensive schools is to be preferred to one made up of a number of small and shrinking schools. And, *faux de mieux*, in the circumstance, such large schools, as Briault suggests (1980, p. 239), may be preferred by most parents. Nevertheless, in the light of the general argument of this book, let us remember that supporters of comprehensive schooling have seen the large school as presenting special difficulties – particularly for the achievement of the ideals of community and fraternity – as well as providing many a headache for those whose responsibility it is to control and administer them.

Pastoral care in the comprehensive school

The increase in the size of secondary schools led to the creation of pastoral systems within them. The purposes of such systems were twofold. First, and broadly, they were to help pupils settle into the schools happily enough; to provide guidance both through the maze of subject options that many schools created for their fourth- and fifth-year pupils, and on jobs and life after school; and to deal with a plethora of personal problems that arise in the day-to-day workings of schools. Second, they were intended to help serve the more ideological purpose of the comprehensive school. Circular 10/65 claimed: 'A comprehensive school aims to establish a school community in which pupils cover the whole ability range and with differing interests and backgrounds can be encouraged to mix with each other, gaining stimulus from the contacts, and learning tolerance and understanding in the process.' (para. 36.) For Shirley Williams this latter aim represents 'The social case for the comprehensive school which has always been unanswerable,' for: 'By educating children of different backgrounds and of different abilities together, comprehensive schools begin to break down class barriers and the mutual ignorance of different social groups, and create the context for a more democratic, open and unprejudiced society.' (1981, p. 156.)

Schools devised ways of breaking down their organisation into smaller, more manageable units – sometimes known as tutor groups. In the selective system the form or class of about thirty pupils had served much the same function, with the form or the class teacher supposedly taking an interest in his pupils that transcended the teaching of some specific subject specialism. This simple way of looking after pupils was not considered wholly satisfactory for comprehensive schools. No doubt, with many teachers, it had been used for little more than the daily registering of pupils, and the collecting of dinner money. And perhaps with many classes little more was necessary. Nevertheless, a teacher did get to know his form in the year or so in which he saw them regularly, and could put even the brief time he met them during the form period to some good use. However, it was believed that comprehensive schools created a greater demand for pastoral care, than could be satisfied by this simple system. In addition, in many comprehensive schools, the complexity of their academic organisation (to be considered more fully in the next chapter) in which children were grouped in diverse ways based upon ability or choice, effectively destroyed the school class as a stable base for pastoral care.

Such tutor groups in turn were the building blocks of still larger units. With a degree of paradox, a number of mainly all-through (11–18) purpose-built comprehensives had developed house systems loosely based upon those of public schools. Some comprehensive schools were too large to meet in a single assembly every day. John Sharp notes of his own Wyndham School, that as 'an obvious piece of economy', 'the school has no place where large numbers can meet: it is not intended to assemble them together' (1973, p. 5). Instead they met in 'house blocks', which could also serve as dining rooms, and places for any activities which required space greater than that of the normal classroom. However, comprehensive school staff were unhappy, in many instances, with this form of organisation. If a 'house' served as a base for early-morning assemblies and as a dining-room later in the day, it was difficult to create within that house the kind of loyalty believed to be a desirable feature of houses in the public schools. Houses are homes to pupils at independent boarding schools in the way that the comprehensive school 'house' could not be to its members.

As an alternative to the house system, most schools have split themselves into upper and lower schools with a division at thirteen or fourteen years. Schools with sixth forms began to detach the pupils in them more sharply from the main part of the school. (Some schools had built special sixth-form units, in which sixth-formers might be permitted the dubious privilege of smoking within the confines of their own common rooms and out of sight of less senior pupils.) In turn, these diverse elements within the school were divided on year lines: this was described as vertical organisation, and as such was particularly useful in schools which were far from purpose-built, as this form of organisation required no specially designed units to accommodate it.

All staff are expected to play some part in these forms of

organisation, and to be responsible for a tutor group. In some systems, staff may retain responsibility for a tutor group for two or more years, following it thus up the school. This has the obvious advantage (and disadvantage in some instances) that staff and pupils will come to know each other well as time goes by. Such a depth of acquaintance is obviously important when providing advice and guidance. A difficulty in practice – particularly up to the mid-1970s – was the mobility of staff. Teachers were often in the schools for too short a time to play a full part in these systems. Inevitably, a hierarchy of staff concerned with this aspect of the life of a school has developed. There are heads of house, and of upper and lower schools; there are year heads, and all their deputies. Indeed, there is little doubt these hierarchies, that parallel those of the subject departments, have provided a career structure within comprehensive schools for displaced secondary modern school staff – who, otherwise, might have suffered in terms of pay and prospects from comprehensive reorganisation.

How successful have these forms of pastoral organisation been in fulfilling the two broad purposes sketched in at the beginning of this section? Before attempting to answer this question it is worth remarking that comprehensive schools, by virtue of their size and the complexity of their organisation, have created at least some of the problems the pastoral systems attempt to resolve. For instance, Maurice Holt (former headmaster of a comprehensive school and an advocate of the principles on which comprehensivisation was based), in a comment on the consequences of option-grouping, observes that: 'In the conventional comprehensive so much that passes for pastoral care in the middle school is little more than horse-trading over options, but with serious implications for the child when key subjects are dropped.' (1978, p. 175.) In addition, pastoral care demands time and scarce resources that might otherwise be used for teaching. To quote Holt again: 'There is no doubt that in many comprehensive schools, pastoral care has been seen out of perspective, and diverted teaching time and money from curriculum activities.' (1978, p. 168.)

Perhaps evaluation of the pastoral side – in so far as it is concerned with matters of guidance and counselling – is difficult indeed. If there are problems in assessing the worth of much teaching in schools, *a fortiori*, how much greater that difficulty is when we consider their more pastoral concerns. Yet if only because, as Holt remarks, the provision of pastoral work can 'absorb a substantial proportion of promotion points and teaching-time allocation', and 'if only because resources in a school are limited, and likely to become more so, it is necessary to look at the extent of each kind of provision and consider its effectiveness' (1978, p. 16). One major area of difficulty is the vagueness of pastoral work. Is its focus the individual pupil in the school: his or her concerns placed before much else? When such a focus is largely on those coping least well with school life, and behaving badly in the school as a consequence, their counsellors may be open to this criticism by headmaster Peter Dawson: 'It is a characteristic of some of those who work on the pastoral side in large schools that they allow concern for the miscreant to overrule all other considerations' (1982, p. 3).

Holt suggests that pastoral work in schools aims 'to help pupils find a sense of identity': presumably a matter of difficulty for some pupils in the large comprehensive school, for in a back-handed compliment to selective schools he remarks: 'A pupil in a rigidly streamed formal grammar school can at least get his bearings.' (1978, p. 166.) To this end of providing 'a sense of identity', apparently missing for some pupils in the comprehensive school, teachers in Britain have begun to employ methods of guidance and counselling developed originally in the USA: as Trefor Vaughan points out, 'The acceptance of new ideas in guidance and the rise in the number of careers teachers, and the emergence of the counsellor, as a new figure in schools, coincide closely with the rise of comprehensive schools.' (1975, p. 19.) Indeed Vaughan suggests that comprehensive schools have 'extended deep into adolescence the problems of educational and personal choice' (p. 20). He argues, along lines similar to those of Holt, that 'in the larger schools, a sense of uncertainty, even of being lost, can easily emerge, and for the young pupils grow to formidable proportions among so many new faces, both of pupils and staff, most of them strangers' (p. 20).

It is difficult to suppress the thought that this picture of children, isolated and lost at school, is a little too luridly painted, no doubt in the interests of those promoting the virtues of their particular nostrum of guidance and counselling. But if the picture is a fair one, what of the cure? No doubt it is unfeelingly philistine to question, but is guidance and counselling sound enough in theory and practice to correct the social and psychological malaise amongst the young which its practitioners diagnose? My scepticism about a positive answer to this far from rhetorical question is encouraged by the following definition of counselling, culled from a volume entitled *Research in Counselling* (1968):

Counselling is a relationship involving verbal interaction between a professionally trained person and an individual or group of individuals voluntarily seeking help with a problem which is psychological in nature, for the purpose of effecting a change in the individuals seeking help. (Patterson, 1968, p. 82).

The conclusion may be that the effectiveness of pastoral work cannot be measured. However, HMIs in their report on and survey of secondary schooling, and commenting on the provision of pastoral care, claimed that only: 'one-sixth (of their sample of schools) were assessed very favourably in this respect' (1979, p. 238); and that: 'There were on the other hand an equal number of schools where the provision for the personal and social development of pupils was assessed as unsatisfactory.' (p. 238.) In a conclusion suggesting that pastoral care is not altogether effective, the HMIs report observes: 'Overall, the response of pupils of all abilities was judged to be better than the provision made for them.' (1979, p. 238.) No doubt, remarks of this kind may be interpreted to suggest that there be more provision for pastoral care not less. Yet, with a more than equal plausibility, it may be argued that: if it is large schools with their complex organisations that create the psychological and social ills pastoral care is to correct, it might be both cheaper and more effective to reduce the size of schools, and thereby reduce the complexity of their organisation – a suggestion that strikes hard at the comprehensive school itself.

So far I have discussed pastoral care in terms of its fulfilling its first broad aim of accommodating pupils to large schools with complex organisations. Perhaps this is all that can reasonably be demanded of pastoral care. Nevertheless, house and year systems, and the like, were expected to assist in what I earlier dubbed an ideological purpose of comprehensive schooling: 'to break down class barriers and the mutual ignorance of different social groups, and create the context for a more democratic, open and unprejudiced society' (Williams, 1981, p. 156). How successful are and can comprehensive schools be in terms of this particular aim?

Once more, and no doubt rather tediously, it must be remarked that in all too few comprehensive schools is there that desirable 'social mix' without which the attempt 'to break down class barriers' will make no sense. If a comprehensive school, sited in the midst of local authority housing contains largely the sons and daughters of unskilled and semi-skilled manual workers, there are precious few 'class barriers' to break down. Supporters of comprehensive schooling are well aware of this difficulty, but regard evidence for it as showing once again, not the failure of comprehensive schooling *per se*, but the failure of governments and local authorities to pursue the ends of comprehensive schooling with sufficient vigour.

Nor ought we to overlook the all too often unquestioned assumption in the argument advanced by Shirley Williams that schools should break down 'class barriers', and reduce the mutual ignorance of different social groups. Schools are distinguished as social institutions by the fact that they are set up to teach children at least certain basic skills – perhaps to educate them – rather in the same way that hospitals are created for the specific end of curing people. In so far as what Shirley Williams wants can be achieved by such teaching, all well and good. And, indeed, much that is taught in secondary schools may help to reduce the ignorance of pupils of a diversity of social groups. But why this educational purpose is achieved necessarily 'by educating children of different backgrounds and of different abilities together' is far from clear. Indeed, children may well learn reasoned tolerance (where this is justified) of different social groups when they are taught alongside children whose ability and social background are not all that different from their own. Bringing children 'of different backgrounds and abilities together', particularly when both parents and pupils are unhappy or even downright hostile to such compulsory comprehensivisation, may lead to the heightening of 'class barriers', and an increase in mutual ignorance and intolerance.

What little evidence there is on the success of this policy is, anyway, not very encouraging to the supporters of comprehensive reorganisation. Consider, for instance, the research of Julienne Ford, reported in *Social Class and the Comprehensive School*, and concerned to explore 'the reasoning behind the notion that comprehensive reform will produce the "Fairer Society", and investigate the *empirical* validity of assumption involved' (1969, p. viii). She compared three schools: a comprehensive, grammar, and secondary modern. Many of the points she makes in her book, despite its being written from a declared socialist outlook and in that period when comprehensive reorganisation was but 'half-way there', presage points I am making in this work – which views secondary school reform with the inestimable benefits of hindsight. For example, she suggests, that: 'consciousness of class, as this is manifest in aspirations, interaction and subjective models of stratified society, persists in the comprehensive as in the grammar and secondary modern schools' (Ford, p. 123).

Ford asked the question: do academic streams *or* house tutor groups within comprehensive schools have the greatest influence on social mixing? Albeit only in a consideration of the three schools making up her sample, she claims: 'that children in all the streams of all the schools are more likely to choose their "one real friend" from their own form or stream or its equivalent than any other in the same school' (Ford, p. 80). In the comprehensive school in her sample, however, there was no preference for friends in the same house, and the relation of friendship choice to house membership was no more than random. Ford notes that classes in which children spend much of their time are the most genuine social units, and such groups 'tend towards social homogeneity in terms of both class background and the future aspiration of their members' (p. 83). Indeed, Ford claims that the evidence from her sample suggests 'if any type of schooling diminishes the likelihood of class bias in informal relations within the classroom this is not the comprehensive but the grammar school' (p. 103).

Despots and democrats

Another aspect of school life that required to be reformed along lines consistent with the comprehensive principle was the relationship between the teachers and the taught. At least for some supporters of comprehensive schooling, this relationship was to approach one of equality.

Traditionally, schools underlined differences between the teachers and their pupils. Teachers spoke and questioned, and their pupils listened and answered. In contrast, P. E. Daunt argued that in a comprehensive school there will be established a 'co-operative style of discipline' that 'will look notably different from the competitive and authoritarian style to which we are accustomed'. Well aware that such a statement of intent may be greeted with ill-disguised scepticism as to the efficacy of the 'co-operative style of discipline', Daunt adds: 'It will therefore appear to represent a failure of discipline in traditional terms, so that unless its purpose and positive merits are repeatedly explained it will be taken by many people to be a failure and nothing else.' (1975, p. 75.) It must be said that despite much repeated explanation of the purpose and positive merits of the 'co-operative style of discipline', few comprehensive schools have embraced it wholeheartedly. However, those schools, such as Countesthorpe College, that have approached this ideal most closely, are worth considering. As Professor Brian Simon observed of Countesthorpe, it 'is of value as a prototype of the school of the future' (1977, p. 25); and one in which there 'is the emphasis on developing new forms of teacher–pupil relations' (1977, p. 22).

What characterises a 'co-operative style of discipline' which, presumably, was to underpin these 'new forms of teacher–pupil relations'? Certainly the abandonment of traditional ways of establishing discipline within schools, which typically have employed the carrot of reward (in particular success in examinations), and the stick of rebuke and punishment. For example, John Sharp, when headmaster of Wyndham School, argued that 'Cherished traditions may be unhelpful in this respect if they include demands for conformity, a greater care for "standards" than for free growth, and hierarchical attitudes.' (1973, p. 21.) What a turn-about of the conventional outlook of a headmaster it is to find Sharp rejecting the notion of the school as 'A world of petty rules, some based merely on tradition and others on regimentation, enforced by an authority which is, in the last resort, arbitrary and self-perpetuating . . .' (1973, p. 12).

Countesthorpe College, Leicestershire, achieved educational fame in the early 1970s in its attempt to embody in practice the ideal of co-operative discipline. Professor Simon notes: 'Countesthorpe was originally designed as a community college, a focus of youth and adult educational activities as well as a school.' (1977, p. 18.) Very nearly everything about this school was an innovation as far as the state system of education was concerned – although some of the educational notions it embodied have been developed in the context of small independent and private schools such as A. S. Neill's school, Summerhill. Countesthorpe College was part of the 'Leicestershire model' of secondary organisation, and was intended to provide accommodation for 1,500 'students' (as its pupils were pointedly redescribed) between the ages of fourteen and eighteen. Its buildings were of a new and original design. Michael Storm, at the time a principal lecturer at Berkshire College of Education, in an article commissioned by that journal for the discerning parent, *Where*, describes the plan of Countesthorpe as looking 'rather like a diagram of a whirlwind with a central vacuum', and wrote that the buildings 'have an environmental impact similar to that of a light industrial estate or an out-of-town shopping centre' (1973, p. 108).

Countesthorpe's beginning was unpropitious: its early intake was unbalanced and was made up of many 'students' whose stay in the school was to be little more than a year. Its first principal resigned on the grounds of ill-health after only eighteen months at the school. Despite this unfortunate start, it is clear that the school's enthusiastic and radical staff were not to be deterred from attempting to develop (in Simon's phrase) 'new forms of teacher–pupil relations'. Whatever, the positive consequences of such relations, Virginia Makins, an educational journalist, in a contribution to *The Countesthorpe Experience, the First Five Years*, observed that in the school's second year: 'Children wandered around the school, no one knew where they belonged or where to send them, teachers were too wary of resorting to old authoritarian methods.' (1977, p. 35.) This reluctance to resort to old authoritarian methods – arbitrary, traditional and leading to the regimentation that restricts the free growth of the child – may be commendable. However, it could well have contributed to a state of affairs such that, as Makins reports: 'Gradually, damage and graffiti increased until the look of the school seemed to justify the most hostile headlines in the *Leicester Mercury.*' (1977, p. 35.) Nevertheless, Makins admires the way 'the staff's nerve held when it came to avoiding arbitrary rules and sanctions' (1977, p. 50). One such arbitrary rule avoided was refusing pupils permission to play their transistors in school. It might be wondered how much school work can be done accompanied by the broadcasting from transistors. Whether such permissiveness is to be admired may be questioned. To refuse to create and enforce rules merely because they are a matter of arbitration (and authority) is likely to lead to that chaos and disorder which severely restricts the 'free growth of the child'.

And, whilst children are not to be regimented and restrained, what of their parents? For as Makins admits, 'The early history of the school raises some uncomfortable questions.' Amongst such uncomfortable questions is one touching yet again on parental choice: 'Should parents virtually be forced to send children to a school that sets out to be different?' (1977, p. 40.) For example, Storm noted that 'the observance of 'normal attendance hours' is one of several points at which the student-centred world of Countesthorpe is occasionally at odds with the world outside, and local residents, have been quick to note irregular comings and goings' (1973, p. 109). Demonstrating that, for at least one supporter of comprehensive schooling, liberty is not a seamless web, Makins answers her own most pertinent question declaring that: 'too much attention to parents' wishes – in matters ranging from uniforms and rules and corporal punishment to teaching methods and homework – may well, in fact, prevent teachers doing the best possible job of educating the greatest number of children' (1977, p. 41).

How well Countesthorpe went about this 'job of educating the greatest number of children' may, in part, be judged from an address, given by its principal, John Watts, to a meeting of parents in June 1974. The school had been so publically criticised as to have invited an interim inspection by HMIs. Although reports of such inspections were at that time confidential, some of the details of the Countesthorpe report had become common knowledge. In his talk to parents, and in an effort no doubt to rebuild their confidence in the school, Watts reported that the HMIs had commended the staff 'for their dedication to students' welfare and the warmth and trust of their relationships' (1977, p. 150). Alas, Watts had also to report that, despite this dedication and trust 'misbehaviour by students was under inadequate control'. And, sadly the very openness of the school library, with its seven different exits, resulted in 'heavy losses of books until it was removed to an area where it was secure but inadequately housed' (p. 149). Watts summed up this particular stage in the history of the school in this way: 'too many innovations may have been introduced at once' (p. 149).

Countesthorpe, also, was a pioneer in new forms of relations between the head of the school ('principal' at Countesthorpe) and the staff. Traditionally, a headteacher of either sex is an absolute despot. Custom and educational law support the head in his rule – however the nature of such authority may be disguised. In the eyes of many teachers a 'strong' head is one that fulfils this role most completely, and the 'weak' head one that fails miserably to exercise his power adequately. Of course, this absolute despot is expected to rule wisely and judiciously – indeed to consult with colleagues and to seek advice. The 'strong' head is marked out by confidence and assurance that freely enables him to look for such guidance and help. Nevertheless, he is in charge and takes the fullest responsibility for the successes and the failures of his school.

Such a view of the head's role was not acceptable to some supporters of comprehensive reorganisation. It smacked too much of tradition. In contrast, the school was to be run 'democratically': an approach which could be justified in terms of preparing pupils for a democratic society. At Countesthorpe, according to John Watts, 'Authority resides in the collective, the Moot and its subdivisions.' (1981, p. 151.) The Moot, as a general assembly, was open to all teachers, some students, parents, and certain other representatives of the local community. The rule of the one will be replaced by the rule of the many, for: 'The Head will have shed power, not just to the point of careful consultation, but having agreed not to overrule the staff and further still, to abide by and operate on their consensus.' (1981, p. 96.)

The advantage of this form of organisation is that nearly everyone affected by decisions takes some part (although individually this may be small) in making them. As Watts puts it, the authority of the collective 'is all the more effective for being an authority conferred by those upon whom it is binding' (1981, p. 151). But are decisions arrived at by the many necessarily any more wise and sensible than those arrived at by a competent headteacher? Experience suggests otherwise. Indeed, the authority of the collective may be greater and more awesome than that of a single individual. Those of an anti-authoritarian disposition, perhaps, ought to think twice before handing over authority to collectives. Such authority may be less restrained and accountable than that exercised by responsible individuals.

There are other more mundane objections to this way of running a school. As Professor Robin Pedley points out: the many committees of Countesthorpe, the sharing of administrative duties, 'together with the business of running the place and the need for everyone to be consulted about virtually everything, mean that an immense amount of time is taken up in exhaustive and exhausting discussions' (1978, p. 129). Former headmaster, Peter Dawson, sums up this type of objection succinctly: 'Reaching decisions by the consensus approach is only possible in two ways: by having staff spend long hours in meetings after school, or by reducing teaching programmes so that discussions take place while the school is in session.' (1981, p. 180.) It is then not surprising to read Storm's comment that Countesthorpe (at least in the early 1970s) was 'absolutely ideal for the radical young teacher, interested in experimentation, and with a burning faith in the power of educational institutions to transform society' (1973, p. 112).

What of teachers who are not so young, not so radical? Sharp observes reasonably enough, and with his own experience as an innovatory headmaster no doubt in mind, 'the educationist cannot work out his dream world until he has persuaded others that it is feasible' (1973, p. 103). But if persuasion fails, what then? The suspicion is that there will be recourse to those traditional powers of the head to shape and re-shape the school to his will and liking. There is evidence that innovating and democratically-minded heads have become impatient with their all too cautious and conservative staff. For instance, Pedley remarks that in schools where mixed-ability teaching has been introduced, 'it is the head of the school who is usually the innovator, and too often he fails to allow for the natural self-doubt in some members of staff' (1978, p. 12).

Another approach, that was suggested to resolve the dilemma of the democratic yet radical supporter of comprehensive organisation, was to reform teachers: to transform them from conservative opponents of educational change. For instance, Nanette Whitbread, a senior lecturer at Leicester College of Education, and an assistant editor of *Forum*, at a *Forum*/Comprehensive Schools Committee called for 'a fundamental change in teacher attitudes'. (Reported by Waters.) For colleges of education, 'this required a process of de-indoctrination of students who were themselves still mostly the products of grammar schools'. (Waters, in *Forum*.) This outlook was put even more forcefully by Eric Midwinter in his advocacy of in-service training for teachers based upon teacher centres. All teachers would be encouraged to embrace 'total comprehensivisation with non-streaming and all the frills. . . . It would mean anything up to 5,000 teachers requiring a complete re-direction in their roles and attitudes' (Midwinter, 1974, p. 10). However, judging from polls of teacher attitudes there is little evidence that, despite de-indoctrination, there has been all that much change in teacher attitudes to 'total comprehensivisation with non-streaming and all the frills'.

The more extreme forms of democracy, and equalitarian relations between staff and pupils, have been introduced into few state schools. These approaches require a young and radical staff prepared to devote considerable amounts of time and energy to school affairs – often above and beyond that required in teaching their pupils. Also, the schools like Countesthorpe may come to incur (as had Risinghill School in the 1960s) the hostility of parents and the local community, and the all too frequent attentions of the media. Nor is it certain that experiments in novel ways of running schools, and 'new forms of teacher–pupil relations', will be successful – judging from the early history of Countesthorpe College. It is, then, not surprising that relatively few schools have emulated the model of schooling embodied in Countesthorpe. Indeed, some (perhaps most) comprehensive schools have been run on staunchly traditional lines. Eltham Green School, whose 'road out of bomb alley' has been entertainingly described by its headmaster Peter Dawson, is one such school.

It would be illiberal to deny to radical young teachers the opportunity to create schools organised on non-traditional lines and to develop 'new forms of teacher–pupil relations' – even within the state system. However, it is equally illiberal to force those parents, who are not convinced of the educational virtues of such schools, to send their children to them. Such coercion may become increasingly unlawful, as local authorities begin to take greater note of the implications of Article 2 of the European Convention of Human Rights (signed in 1952 by Britain) which establishes that parents have the right to have their children taught 'in conformity with their religious and philosophical convictions'. (It was recourse to the European Convention of Human Rights which has led recently to a reconsideration of the legality of corporal punishment for the children of parents deeply hostile to this particular sanction.)

It is difficult to decide the extent to which greater democracy in schools, and more equality between teachers and the taught, are part and parcel of comprehensive reorganisation. Some headmasters, such as Peter Dawson, sincerely committed to comprehensive schooling, claim that it is not. To such heads, stress on greater democracy and equality *within* the school is an aberration, perhaps a hangover from the heady 1960s, when so much was heard about the value of liberation from traditional restraints and authority. Nevertheless, there does seem to be a connection between the demand for greater equality and democracy *within* schools and the egalitarianism that provided the ideological impulse for comprehensive reorganisation.

6 The organisation of comprehensive schools: two

'If selection into separate schools at eleven is premature, breeds self-fulfilling prophecies and high rates of failure, selection into separate streams in a common school must surely do the same.' Auriol Stevens, educational correspondent of *The Observer*, 1980.

Selection within the comprehensive school

'Abolish selection!' was the rallying cry of those who wished to reorganise secondary schools on comprehensive lines. What criteria of selection were to be abandoned or abolished was not always made clear. Children must not be selected by ability, but what of by sex, neighbourhood, or religion? The continued existence of single-sex comprehensive schools, in some cases organised in terms of the neighbourhood and/or denominational origins of their children, gave the lie to that. The 1976 Education Act, however, provided legal backing to the notion that, in a comprehensive school, children were not to be selected on the grounds of ability – despite, thereby, making it all the more difficult for such schools to achieve that range of ability and appropriate 'social mix' without which (at least for some supporters of reorganisation) no school could be truly comprehensive.

Furthermore, if schools could not select their intakes by ability, how were they to allocate their pupils to teaching groups? The now repealed 1976 Education Act provides no answer to this all-important question. For Professor Pedley, however, 'to transfer selection from outside the school to inside the school still entails rejection for the great majority of children and the thwarting of many parental hopes . . .' (1978, p. 104). Headmaster and educational consultant, Maurice Holt put this point in a more picturesque form: 'it is difficult to think of the streamed or banded comprehensive as any less incongruous than a Nash terrace with a thatched roof' (1978, p. 163).

The question of the success or failure of comprehensive schools continues to be posed with respect to the organisation of them, as in the last chapter. Auriol Stevens makes this point well in her book whose title reveals an interest in a neglected minority, *Clever Children in Comprehensive Schools*. She argues: 'If selection into separate schools at eleven is premature, breeds self-fulfilling prophecies and high rates of failure, selection into separate streams in a common school must surely do the same.' (1980, p. 28.) Her logic is faultless, but presents the possibility – surely of concern to a supporter of comprehensive schools like herself – that if her conclusion is false, so is her premise: 'selection into separate schools at eleven is premature'. And yet she adds, in a comment upon the form of teaching that is the preferred alternative to 'selection into separate streams', 'In practice, mixed ability teaching does not work so well.' (1980, p. 30.) If, indeed, this is the truth as matter of undisputed fact, then comprehensive schooling looks like being shown up as a sham.

Streaming, setting, and banding are all terms of educational art that describe different practices of grouping children by ability and aptitude. a streamed intake is a year group divided by assessed ability of the most general kind into teaching groups. An intake which is 'set' is grouped by ability and aptitude within a particular subject. An intake that is 'banded' is divided into (usually) three groups or bands, on the grounds of ability-groups, which in their turn may be divided in diverse ways.

If comprehensive schools find it impossible, as a matter of practice, to avoid streaming, setting or banding, what then? May we conclude that, contrary to the claims of those who advocated their creation, comprehensives do not abolish selection? Do they rather, in Pedley's words (see above), 'transfer selection from outside the school to inside the school'? The consequence – 'rejection for the great majority of children and the thwarting of many parental hopes' – is what comprehensive schools were established to end forever.

It certainly will not do to fudge the issue, as does Maurice Holt, by arguing that: 'It is often forgotten that all groups – even the most rigidly streamed – are mixed ability groups ...' (1978, p. 164). If this were truly the case, there would be no case to answer. No doubt, Holt is correct in his insight that, even with a group of children selected and sorted with the greatest of care to make up as homogeneous a group on the grounds of (say) general intellectual ability as human judgement can allow, no one of these children is literally a clone of another. For, children who are alike in one respect are dissimilar in other respects. What we are concerned with here is the principle of selecting pupils for groups by some feature that all its pupil members share to some degree. Pedley and others are surely right in their expressed belief that any other way of teaching children other than individually, or in mixed ability groups, subverts the comprehensive school.

Consider then a report of a survey of teacher attitudes and responses to mixed ability in: *Mixed Ability Teaching: Problems and Possibilities.* Margaret Reid, and her fellow researchers, interviewed 479 teachers from 29 schools selected by virtue of 'being comprehensive schools with experience of mixed-ability grouping for all or part of the curriculum in the early years of secondary education at least' (1981, p. 14). This study does not attempt to judge the success of mixed-ability teaching relative to streamed or setted classes. However, Reid points out that 'studies so far carried out which have sought to make direct comparison of streamed and unstreamed groups have been inconclusive in their findings – a fact too readily glossed over by some proponents of mixed-ability teaching' (1981, p. 8). Despite the inconclusive character of such findings, a number of comprehensive schools have introduced mixed-ability teaching, at least in the first one or two years of secondary schooling. This report of the NFER's 'Mixed Ability Teaching Project' asks most pertinently: Why?

In many cases, it seems, largely because the headmaster thought it a good thing. Reid's report refers to the 'directive mode' when the 'decision to introduce mixed-ability groups lies wholly or mainly with the head' (1981, p. 28). This was the approach adopted in over two-thirds of the schools visited by the researchers. (So much, one might reflect, for democracy and equality within the comprehensive school!) The report gives as an example of the 'directive mode', one school whose head decided 'completely authoritatively' (his words) to introduce non-streaming throughout the school. The head recalled that '70–80 per cent of the staff were "apprehensive"' (Reid, 1981, p. 29). Given, as in the view of Pedley (1978, p. 106), that for mixed-ability teaching 'to be successful and effective day after day throughout the year, the teacher must be physically fit and endowed with considerable reserves of energy – comparable, let us say, to those required by successful Prime Ministers', such apprehension is understandable. The head in question claimed that three years later a survey of his staff revealed only one teacher hostile to mixed-ability teaching. The researchers, however, note that this school had one of the highest turnovers of staff in the study; and of teachers sampled at this particular school, 'there were a number who were unconvinced as to the merits of unstreaming' (Reid, 1981, p. 30). Making a more general point of schools in the sample, Reid, *et al,* observed that: 'in no case were parents' views sought concerning the grouping practices to be adopted' (p. 42).

Of those 403 teachers teaching mainly mixed-ability classes, 92 per cent saw *some* advantage to pupils in mixed-ability classes, although almost one-fifth saw no advantages for themselves. 'In contrast, teachers wholly or mainly concerned with streamed, setted or banded classes almost always perceived these methods of organisation as of advantage to both pupils and teachers.' (Reid, 1981, p. 66.) What were the advantages of mixed-ability teaching for pupils? Reid, *et al*, note that such a form of class organisation was seen to avoid 'labelling'. To label children is now a cardinal sin in some educational circles. Yet, whilst to label (or categorise) children unsympathetically or dogmatically is not to be supported, some form of classification is logically unavoidable in the relationship between the teacher and the taught – beginning with conceiving children as 'pupils'. Indeed, the report notes 'how frequently teachers who condemned labelling went on to talk of their pupils in terms of those that were 'less able', 'more able' and 'average', implying that these were recognisable and discrete groups within their classrooms . . .' (Reid, 1981, p. 71). Indeed, in discussion of their findings, Reid, *et al*, employ these general categories too: themselves 'implying that these were recognisable and discrete groups' within their respondents' classrooms.

Another advantage seen by teachers in mixed-ability classes was that they permitted a fresh start for pupils at the school. However, the report suggested that the advocates of a clean slate for eleven year olds 'may simply be disguising poor liaison with primary schools, and taking insufficient account of the very real differences which exist in the interests and abilities of eleven-year-old children' (Reid, 1981, p. 155).

The reduction of behaviour problems was seen by 29 per cent as an advantage for the teachers of mixed-ability classes. The report quotes a head of a mathematics department in a large urban school who noted pragmatically: 'We do not have enough teachers who can keep order – unstreamed classes overcome this.' (Reid, 1981, p. 75.) Is this yet another illustration of the comprehensive school attempting to remedy the ills its size and complex organisation create? Grammar and secondary modern schools were not free of 'behaviour problems' as indiscipline is typically described today. But their smaller scale and different concerns may have helped to make their problems more manageable. A large comprehensive school of 1,000 pupils or more – particularly if its intake contains a proportionately high percentage of less able pupils – is likely to have a sizeable number of pupils for whom school is more an experience of failure than success. Indeed, as we shall see, the very demand that a comprehensive school provide a curriculum suitable for all pupils – despite their range of abilities and aptitudes – may make it more difficult to provide adequately for less able pupils. The temptation is then to try to spread the least able throughout the school for fear that they otherwise become a cohesive and delinquent group hostile to everything the school stands for. Reid, *et al*, however, do ask the question: if mixed-ability classes are so valuable for maintaining order, why is this form of organisation largely abandoned by most schools in the third and fourth years – perhaps the years when there are the greatest 'behaviour problems'?

Given, then, that unstreamed classes may help teachers to keep order, what specifically educational advantages do they have? Reid, *et al*, note: 'Almost a quarter of those substantially involved with mixed-ability classes associated their difficulties in teaching such groups with meeting the needs of the less able.' (1981, p. 86.) Indeed, 45 per cent of teachers identified disadvantages for less able children arising from the fact that teaching was aimed at the middle of the classes. The researchers quote an experienced remedial teacher, who, whilst repeating the conventional wisdom that segregation was in many respects reprehensible, admitted 'it did cater for the less able academically' (Reid, 1981, p. 86). This same remedial teacher 'pointed out that in many mixed-ability classes "teachers are often unwilling and unable to do this"' (p. 86).

If some teachers saw mixed-ability classes as unsuitable for the least able, nearly six out of ten teachers sampled considered that such classes led 'to a reduction in the motivation and achievement of the more able' (p. 95). Reid, *et al*, noted that the attainments (or lack of them) of the more able in mixed-ability classes was the subject of extensive comment by teachers. Teachers expressed 'concern over a lack of "academic texture" and the view that in such classes able children would not be extended' (1981, p. 82). This disadvantage of mixed-ability classes has led headmaster Peter Dawson to the conclusion: 'It is no more excusable to leave the best young scientific minds in the country to make the most of it in a mixed-ability physics group than it is to give them all the attention and applause.' (1981, p. 55.)

For all the suggestion made that, in mixed-ability classes, teachers aim for the middle, Reid, *et al*, express some anxiety about the lack of comment on average children from their sample. The report (p. 95) refers to 'the danger of the possibility of "average" children being overlooked and the range of their individual differences being ignored' as a result of a concern for the needs of both the least and the most able in mixed-ability classes. This is a possibility that Dawson suggests may be present generally in the comprehensive school: 'Paradoxically, the normal child's needs are not infrequently neglected while attention is given to those with profound problems.' (1981, p. 110.) The paradox leads Dawson to conjecture: 'If a comprehensive school is only able to control the miscreant, stretch the high flyer and support the backward by neglecting the ordinary pupils who fall into none of these categories, going comprehensive has all been a ghastly mistake.' (1981, p. 107.)

Mixed-ability teaching aims to answer the demand that comprehensive schools refuse to categorise pupils, but ought rather to treat individual pupils on their own merits (or demerits). For such teaching, according to Alfred Yates, chairman of the NFER's 'Mixed Ability Teaching Project', 'involves the attempt so to fashion or adapt teaching methods and approaches as to make due allowance for the individual needs and capabilities of each pupil'. (Reid, 1981, p. xiii.) Reid, *et al*, however, found that whole-class teaching was 'very frequently used by the majority of teachers of mixed-ability classes, although the extent of its use in lessons clearly varied . . .' (1981, p. 88). Yet, whole-class teaching is the antithesis of the mixed-ability approach as defined by Yates. One head of a technical studies department is reported as denying the possibility of any other method than that of whole-class teaching: 'You must class teach, you can't have 25 to 35 pupils all doing different work' (Reid, 1981, p. 88).

In contrast, the HMIs' 1979 survey of schools criticises the attempts to cope with the individual needs of pupils by the use of 'worksheets'. In some schools, worksheets have largely replaced textbooks. Although they place a large burden on the reprographics resources of a school, worksheets are a boon to the hard-pressed teacher of mixed-ability classes. These sheets can be filled with questions and examples to be worked so as (in theory) to keep both the least and the most able busy for the lesson's duration. In addition, their use is at least a nod in the direction of making 'allowance for the individual needs and capabilities of each pupil', as well as reducing the necessity for general exposition to the whole class. However, such a method is as open to abuse as is any other; the HMIs noted that: 'Reading material [in the form of] the worksheets frequently provided for mixed-ability classes, was rarely differentiated in linguistic difficulty, and pupils of widely varying abilities were sometimes expected to be able to assimilate quantities of information to be stored in files and reproduced in test and examinations.' (1979, p. 73.)

Given their full exploration of the pros and cons of mixed-ability teaching, it is not surprising that Reid, *et al*, came to the anodyne conclusion that 'there is no one best way of organising pupils for all purposes' (1981, p. 146). How pupils are organised (or organise themselves) necessarily depends upon circumstances and purposes. If Whitegrove school wishes to beat Blackdale school at soccer, it will pick the best team for that purpose. If we are playing 'fun' football with no concern about winning or losing then criteria for inclusion in the team can be radically different. Much the same goes for organising classes for academic pursuits as it does for athletics and games. How we organise our classes depends upon our ends in view. For instance, those mathematics teachers, interviewed by Reid, *et al*, who 'saw their subject as comprising a given body of knowledge which required an ordered method of exploration . . . did not generally perceive their subject as well suited to a mixed-ability approach' (1981, p. 130). And, for perhaps similar reasons, 'the majority [of modern language teachers] considered that mixed-ability language work was neither desirable nor feasible' (Reid, 1981, p. 136). Where, however, the purpose is not (say) progress through a carefully structured mathematics syllabus,. or the incremental development of linguistic skills, then mixed-ability groups may be an appropriate way of organising the class. It all depends, once again, on the ends in view, the purposes to be fulfilled. For example, Reid, *et al*, note that the highest approval for mixed-ability classes comes from those teachers employing the method of discussion to pursue studies rather vaguely entitled 'Humanities'. How much time a school can devote to such studies (despite their genuine value), however, is a moot point; probably, in fact, rather little.

The above view of mixed ability teaching seems widely shared by most secondary schools. A survey, carried out by the NFER in 1974–75 of over 1,000 comprehensive schools, revealed that 55 per cent of them used mixed-ability grouping in the first year. In 1980, in schools sampled by the NFER, this figure was unchanged. Nevertheless, whilst, in 1975, a quarter of the schools still retained mixed-ability in the third year, by 1980 this percentage had dropped to 18 per cent; 66 per cent of the schools in the sample were setting, streaming or banding and the remaining 16 per cent were using no single grouping arrangement. Such findings are supported by those of the HMIs' survey, reporting that out of the 365 schools sampled, only 34 used mixed ability throughout the school; and 'Of the 34 schools only four had to provide for the full range of ability'. (1979, p. 96.)

The general picture is that just over half our comprehensive schools probably employ mixed-ability grouping in the first year. Indeed, given the paucity of information on their pupil intakes (so helpful for making a 'fresh start') and the variable standards and attainments achieved in the feeder primary schools, one might be struck that only just over half of the schools are using this approach. Yet by the third year, perhaps only one in five schools still employs mixed-ability grouping – and the numbers of such schools may be falling as a consequence of increased teacher, parent, and pupil dissatisfaction with this form of grouping as an aid to teaching and learning.

No doubt some schools will continue with mixed-ability teaching so long as they have a headmaster such as one quoted by Reid, *et al*, who argued that: 'Unstreaming is socially desirable; you shouldn't have all the kids with dirty vests in one form'. Such unstreaming, it appears, is socially desirable – despite the fact, admitted by this egalitarian headmaster, that: '. . . the abler [pupils] would get on faster if they were streamed' (1981, p. 25). It comes then as no surprise, given the existence of such sentiments, that Reid, *et al*, found one teacher who declared: 'We shall continue with mixed-ability, despite your findings, because that is the system we believe in.' (1981, p. 10.) However, given the many doubts of most teachers of the general efficacy of mixed-ability grouping, setting, streaming, and banding are likely to remain the main ways by which pupils are organised for teaching purposes. And given the propensity, noted by Reid, *et al*, for teachers to categorise their pupils as 'less able', 'average' and 'more able', it seems as if selection will not be eliminated from mixed-ability groups either – however desirable it is to encourage 'individualised learning' within them. It looks as if comprehensive schools have failed to abolish selection after all.

Comprehensive curriculum

One further reason for selection within comprehensive schools is that the existence of option choices in the third, fourth and fifth years makes it necessary. For as the HMIs' survey, *Aspects of Secondary Education in England*, makes abundantly clear: 'up to the age of 14 all pupils within a school study substantially the same programme of subjects. . . . In the vast majority of schools the structure of the curriculum then undergoes a major change: the number of subjects which are studied by all pupils is reduced considerably and much of their programmes are drawn from an often large and nearly always complex system of options.' (1979,

p. 14.) And, as Holt notes, with the consequence that: 'Entry to option subjects is usually conditional on staff recommendations, and always on the number of staff and places available so that it is no surprise to discover that the old tripartite structure is alive and well and living in the option columns.' (1978, p. 13.) The curriculum of the comprehensive school then, strongly differentiates between pupils at least by the age of thirteen. As David Hargreaves, University Reader in Education at Oxford, remarks, 'The present system has replaced the old eleven-plus with a new selective test – the thirteen-plus when pupils are allocated to the three bands of 'O' level, CSE and non-examination groups.' (1982, p. 165.) How has this strikingly non-egalitarian curriculum come to be established within the comprehensive school?

One reason is the intensely individualistic view of the curriculum held by some supporters of comprehensive reorganisation. This particular view of the curriculum is put directly and succinctly by Professor Pedley: 'The curriculum, i.e. the child's programme of activities, should arise out of his needs and be essentially peculiar to him.' (1978, p. 166.) In this view of what ought to be taught in schools, children are unique individuals with greatly differing abilities, capacities and aptitudes. As a matter of practical pedagogic necessity that fact has led schools to sort and sift pupils into streams and sets: however difficult and provisional the judgements required. But for Pedley, and other supporters of comprehensive reform, such practices smack of the odious segregation that reorganisation must bring to an end. If, then, teachers cannot categorise and group children (however provisionally), each child must be treated as the unique individual he is, and provided with his very own individual pattern of studies.

Yet another explanation is that there is a muddle over what ought to be taught in comprehensive schools. Penelope Weston, in her report of research by the SSRC funded '13–14 Curriculum Study', *Framework for the Curriculum*, points out: 'Whereas a grammar school could harness all its energies to a single short term end – ensuring for its pupils every chance of success in a basically academic programme – the school with a non-selective entry had to bear in mind the variety of needs, expectations and goals to be found among its pupil body.' (1977, p. 159.) However, as many a school discovered, creating a curriculum to satisfy such diverse needs within one school has proved a difficult – perhaps impossible – task. For one thing, comprehensive schooling had been sold on the promise that it would provide a grammar school education for all. If the opportunities for academic study found in grammar schools was not provided by comprehensive schools, then the failure of such schools to live up to their promises would be manifest. On the other hand, there were some who spoke up for the curricular provision of the much despised secondary modern. For example, Hargreaves, a supporter of comprehensive schooling, argues that 'The best secondary modern schools avoided two extremes: that of seeing their clients as the unteachable 'rejects' who had to be kept off the streets until they were fifteen, and that of trying to ape the grammar school.' (1982, p. 65.) It is understandable, then, that in an effort to mix chalk and cheese 'comprehensives have tried to assimilate the two existing traditions from the grammar and modern schools' (Holt, 1978, p. 12).

This is obviously an impossible task: for how can these two traditions – one with an emphasis on bookish academic work, and another largely rejecting this approach in favour of one stressing a choice between courses that are practical, realistic, and vocational (see Newsom Report, 1963) – be adequately integrated? As the HMIs' survey points out: 'the establishment of comprehensive schools has not led to any radical reshaping of the curriculum, which essentially continues the practice of the selective schools with some added features taken from the modern schools' (1979, p. 260). Most 11–18 secondary schools therefore abandon, beyond the second year of studies, the attempt to provide a common curriculum, but as an alternative, provide an *à la carte* menu of curriculum items. As the headmasters, Sharp and Holt both note, there are two immediate consequences. One is the necessity to prepare an elaborate timetable to provide opportunities for children to combine as many diverse option choices together as the school's resources and their teachers' ingenuity allow. The second is the necessity to counsel and advise second and third year children as to appropriate option choices – an exercise, as Holt points out (see chapter 5), which demands the allocation of scarce staff time, and diverts teachers from their teaching.

The HMIs' survey points out that a school providing an extensive range of options necessarily creates 'an extremely complex organisation, so complex indeed that one head confessed to being defeated by the organisation' (1979, p. 41). Such may be the complexity of an option system that the HMIs believe: 'It is not always fully understood by teachers, let alone parents.' (p. 41.) Option systems of such complexity inevitably create the logistical problem of ensuring that both teachers and taught arrive at classroom, laboratories, other practical rooms, gymnasia, etc., on time to start a lesson together. David Hargreaves, a seasoned observer of school life, describes the 'Paddington

Station effect', when 'every forty minutes: the bell rings and hordes of pupils pack into the narrow corridors as they search for the next teachers' (1982, p. 89). In contrast, there is the 'Luton Airport effect'; 'the children stream round the building, but are now armed with huge cases, bags, carriers, hold-alls in which all their belongings are kept' (Hargreaves, 1982, p. 89). It takes little imagination to contemplate the impact of such movement (however regulated) on good order and discipline within the school, never mind the fabric of buildings housing the school. These general problems of movement are, of course, as I argued in the preceding chapter, exacerbated by the large size of comprehensive schools.

And yet, despite the range of options on offer, the HMIs' survey suggests that choices effectively available to pupils, or actually taken by them, are not all that wide. It certainly does not 'necessarily result in either a "balanced" programme or one which has coherence for the pupil' (HMI, 1979, p. 260). One example the survey gives of what the HMIs believe to be an unbalanced programme, was of a girl 'with a course consisting of English, mathematics, religious education, physical education, home economics, careers, typing, shorthand and commerce'. This programme may be one (paraphrasing Pedley) arising out of her needs and be essentially peculiar to her, but it might be questioned (it is by the HMIs) as to its balance and coherence. In addition, it is often difficult to know whether such individual programmes do genuinely arise from the needs and interests peculiar to individual pupils; or, rather, arise from what the option system – given some initial choices on the part of pupils – permits them to follow.

Relatively few teachers, parents and pupils are happy with the comprehensive school curriculum as it is now. For example, the HMIs' survey suggests that the least able children have 'less real choice than other pupils' (1979, p. 37). For Hargreaves, the dominance of the grammar school tradition within comprehensive schools makes their curriculum highly unsuitable for average and below-average children. Hargreaves goes so far as to claim that 'comprehensive schools have intentionally obliterated the concept of the modern school and many of the experiments that prospered there' (1982, p. 65). Auriol Stevens argues that 'in the process [of establishing comprehensive schools], straight academic, traditional schooling for clever children has been to some degree neglected.' Stevens gives an example of just such neglect when a 'mixed-sex grammar school in the north-east [of England] which takes children from thirteen to eighteen' went comprehensive: 'As a grammar school, it used to have a fast stream who took

'O' levels early and then spent three years in the sixth form leading to the Oxford and Cambridge entrance exams. In 1978 this group had gone. Greek had gone. Russian had gone. Latin was confined to the sixth form.' (1980, p. 141.)

In summary: the evidence from the HMIs' survey is that 'many people are not well served by the curricular structures and organisations of their schools' (1979, p. 266). Thus, the comprehensive school, in attempting to satisfy 'the variety of needs, expectations and goals to be found among its pupil body' (see Weston, above), has ended by satisfying very few.

Supporters of comprehensive schooling, such as Maurice Holt and David Hargreaves, who are also perceptive critics of what comprehensive schools offer in practice, reject the notion of a curriculum largely based upon multiple choice. Holt, indeed, argues that with such an approach 'There is no curriculum unity; there is no stability to the learning group; and there is no way in which the school can become a total influence system.' (1978, p. 166.) Hargreaves takes a similar view, but opposes most strongly what he describes as the heavy emphasis on 'cognitive-intellectual' studies in the comprehensive school. He knows that comprehensive schools were expected to maintain the grammar school tradition within them. What he believes, and deplores, is that comprehensives have become dominated by ex-grammar school teachers and the grammar school ethos. One suspects there is an element of exaggeration in this latter thesis; but in so far as it is a partial truth, Hargreaves is a little naive in his failure to see this effect as a well-nigh inevitable consequence of comprehensive reorganisation itself.

Non-streaming, and the development of mixed ability classes, are part and parcel of an attempt to put off the evil day of selecting pupils for specifically academic courses. For this reason – and also to disguise the fact that such selection is taking place – the day is sometimes put off until the time comes to choose third year options. But, in the meantime, if only to keep the possibility of options open to all, every pupil must be subjected to the grammar school curriculum. In practice this cannot be; Latin, for example, either goes altogether or is taught to very few. The 11–18 school, in its attempt in the first two years to offer the grammar school curriculum to all, inevitably attenuates and weakens it – hence Auriol Stevens' concern for clever children in comprehensive schools. Nevertheless, the grammar school curriculum, however watered-down, is, as Hargreaves correctly observes, unsuitable fare for many average and below average children.

Holt and Hargreaves draw the proper conclusion that all is not well with what is taught and learnt in comprehensive schools.

But are their prescriptions for cure all that helpful? For instance, Hargreave's 'main proposal is that all secondary schools should have a central, core curriculum, for pupils between the ages of eleven and fourteen and fifteen, which should be organised around community studies and the expressive arts' (1982, p. 128). This certainly removes any heavy emphasis on the 'cognitive-intellectual', but at what cost? First, one suspects, this will sharpen the division between the state and the independent schools, who may, from balance and self-interest stress, even more than they do now, the 'cognitive-intellectual' element in their own curriculum fare. (Indeed, one can imagine the independent schools welcoming Hargreaves' curriculum suggestions for state schools, as being of considerable advantage to themselves.) Second, more formal study of traditional subjects would be delayed for many until the age of fifteen and later. Dr Hargreaves' prescription leads to the replacement of the thirteen-plus by the fifteen-plus. Is this any genuine improvement? Does it not mean that those children who are not firmly supported by home and friends, whilst capable of intellectual study, will be even less likely to move forward to such study than they are now? Subjects, such as maths and languages, are often learnt quite readily by bright youngsters in their early years of schooling. Will it do to delay their rapid progress in these subject areas because of an egalitarian demand that everyone march down the same road at much the same pace? Auriol Stevens answers this question well with her comment: 'Holding children back – "because all can't none shall" – is an unwarranted oppression' (1980, p. 30).

Examinations and profiles

A further reason for selection within the comprehensive schools is that the pattern of examinations demands it. As with the curricula, there was no thought-out approach to examining, assessing, or testing pupils in the comprehensive school. Indeed, nothing so much reveals comprehensive reorganisation as an ill-conceived political expedient, as the fact that there was so little in the way of an educational policy for such schools *after* reorganisation. I have already noted how the politician, C. A. R. Crosland, seemed to conceive of them as simply replicating the tri- or bipartite selective system within their walls. Comprehensive reorganisation, seen from this particular viewpoint, was not a fundamental reform, merely an attempt to disguise the allegedly unpopular fact of selection at eleven-plus.

In practice, the schools employ the two main methods of

examining pupils that had been developed within the selective system. The GCE had grown out of university-based school certificates created in 1918. These examinations served two main purposes: first, as a school leaving certificate, indicating the level of performance in terms of the grammar school curricula; and second, as an indication of capacity for academic study at university and college. Before 1950, the certificate was awarded for adequate competence over a range of subjects. After 1950, certificates were awarded for performance in individual subjects: a reform which helped to undermine the notion of a common curriculum – at least in terms of the grammar school. In contrast, the CSE introduced in 1965, was intended for pupils whose performance in examinations was expected to be intellectually lower than that of the 20 per cent or so entering for the GCE. In addition, the CSE broke fresh ground with its Mode 3 examination which is marked by the teachers of examinees, and moderated (compared with a notional external standard) by outsiders. The GCE has two levels – ordinary and advanced – whilst the CSE is a one level examination.

Thus a comprehensive school could be preparing its pupils for two distinctly different forms of examination. As Pedley writes (1978, p. 101): 'The present GCE 'O' level at sixteen was designed essentially for grammar-school pupils, CSE for those of average and below-average ability in secondary modern and comprehensive schools.' This state of affairs may be defended in terms of providing opportunities for all. In addition, comprehensive schools were anxious to demonstrate that their examination successes were at least as good as those of the selective schools they replaced. As the HMIs' survey points out: 'Rightly or wrongly, examination results were commonly perceived by the school as the sole indicator of its success in the eyes of the community. Newly formed comprehensive schools were liable to be particularly conscious of this pressure.' (1979, p. 248.)

Parental expectations (and those of their children) had, no doubt, been raised by comprehensive schools offering a 'grammar school education for all'. The character of the GCE examination as a single subject examination has probably increased the pressure on schools to enter more and more of its pupils for one or more GCEs. Yet, as the HMIs comment: 'The fact that four out of every five pupils was aiming at a GCE or CSE examination must have meant that for some the course was likely to have been inappropriate since these examinations between them were intended to cater, subject by subject, for the top 60 percentiles of ability.' (1979, p. 34.) These observations are a reminder that there are as yet no public examinations designed to assess the attainments of the least able children in school (in technical jargon those in the bottom 40 percentiles of ability). Pedley's view, then, that the existence of two separate examination systems 'enforces premature division of children within a school between the one path and the other [and] is a standing denial of our faith in the comprehensive principle' (1978, p. 107), under-states the position. Schools direct their pupils down three paths, two of which may lead to examination success, the other to no assessment of any kind.

Offering two sorts of examination systems within one school inevitably makes for considerable logistical and timetabling dif-ficulties. In some schools these problems are compounded as children are entered for more than one GCE board, and examined in more than one 'mode' at CSE. Inevitably, a great deal of scarce staff time and energy goes into organising and invigilating these examinations. The effect of going comprehensive seems to have increased the attention given to examinations rather than les-sened it. The HMIs' survey argues that: 'The very high priority accorded to examinations by schools, parents and employers has effects which far exceed the purposes for which they are designed.' (1979, p. 247.) In order to satisfy parental expectations of examination success raised, in part, by comprehensive re-organisation, schools are under some pressure to enter border-line candidates for examinations. The HMIs point out that, particularly when candidates were such borderline performers, 'the effect was to narrow learning opportunities, especially when work was concentrated on topics thought to be favoured by examiners'. In those latter circumstances, '[sustained] exposition by the teacher and extensive note-taking by the pupil tended to limit oral work . . .' (1979, p. 247).

The irony of it is that supporters of comprehensive schooling are ambivalent about, when not positively hostile to, formal school examinations. The view 'that *all* examinations are in principle educationally unsound and their abolition would automatically permit a "true" education to flourish' is, as de-scribed by Hargreaves, 'The not uncommon "progressive" view', which he nevertheless rejects as a naive and 'unreasoned slogan'. (1982, p. 128.) Storm located this 'progressive' view amongst teachers at Countesthorpe College, where he notes: 'the staff consensus is broadly anti-examination, contrasting with the normal parental preoccupations – for it's the school that's un-usual, not its catchment area' (1973, p. 110). Another expression of the 'progressive' view is found in Daunt's *Comprehensive Values* in which he argues: 'public examinations at 16-plus should be abandoned' (1975, p. 63). In support of this view he argues that examinations inevitably – 'given the hierarchy of numerical or alphabetical grades which examinations entail' (1973, p. 62) – result in some children failing. Such failure, in Daunt's eyes at least, contradicts his 'principle of equal value' (see Chapter 2).

Defenders and opponents of comprehensive schooling are united in believing the present system of examining at sixteen- and eighteen-plus is far from adequate. The DES give cautious support to merging the GCE 'O' level with the CSE so as to provide a common examination for children in the 60 percentiles of the ability range. This much mooted examination reform makes slow progress against a background chorus of doubt and dissent. There are understandable difficulties in bringing together into one unified system two kinds of examinations. In addition, the GCE is controlled by a number of examining boards (loosely based upon a handful of universities) with disparate traditions. Different subject teachers have their own views on the feasibility of creating an examination for such a width of ability. Doubt is expressed that common exam papers are possible for such a wide span of ability without failing to do justice to the most intellectually able children; or, alternatively, demanding too high a level of attainment from the least able candidates. Somewhat outside the debate, but taking a close interest, are two groups. One deplores the fact that advantage is not being taken of the possibility of reform to restructure the curriculum on more radical lines; that would diminish the hegemony of the subject disci- plines (particularly those academic in character) and, as an alternative, promote a more practical and 'integrated' approach to what is taught in schools. The second group points out that sixteen-plus exam reform, on the lines suggested, still leaves the performance of something like 40 per cent of secondary school pupils unassessed and unexamined.

The difficulties involved in reaching agreement over the reform of sixteen-plus examinations, and the administrative, financial, and political problems associated with this projected reorgan- isation, leads some supporters of comprehensive schooling to advocate outright abolition of sixteen-plus exams. For instance, David Hargreaves, whilst, as we have seen, rejecting the view that all examinations are by definition educationally unsound, nevertheless asserts that: 'All the sixteen-plus examinations must be abolished.' (1982, p. 163.) He defends such a draconian measure by arguing that the abolition of the sixteen-plus would put an end to selection at thirteen-plus, 'when pupils are allo- cated to the three bands of 'O' level, CSE, and non-examination groups' (1982, p. 165). Following the abolition of the sixteen-plus exams, according to Hargreaves, 'We could then begin the serious task of improving and increasing – for some already exist – those examinations which assess work-related knowledge and skill and which constitute more genuine occupational qualifications.' (1982, p. 181.)

Would such a measure resolve the dilemmas of comprehensive schooling? This is open to the objections raised against Hargreaves' proposed reform of the curriculum discussed in the preceding section of this chapter: it would increase the gap between private and state schooling. And whilst such an examination might usefully test the majority of children in school, it would not all: particularly those children of an academic and bookish outlook. Its claim to abolish examinations at sixteen may be doubted, for what is involved is the substitution of public examination by school assessment. One wonders whether such a substitution would be welcomed by parents, employers, and bodies such as universities and colleges. The standing of such internally assessed certificates may come to be increasingly dependent upon the reputation of the schools validating them.

It is interesting to note that such a test, with its stress on work-related knowledge and skills, might bring the world of work and that of school closer together. Perhaps this is not a bad thing, but it is somewhat in conflict with Hargreaves' conception of a core curriculum of community studies and the expressive arts. However, Hargreaves objects so strongly to any kind of preparation for employment, other than that specifically linked to it, that he is moved to say: '. . . it must be an offence for an employer to recruit an employee on the basis of the latter's possession of paper qualifications unless it can be demonstrated that these test qualities and skills which are necessary to do the job properly.' (1982, p. 180.) Nothing seems more likely to destroy liberal education in schools and universities than such an authoritarian rule (putting on one side whether it could be applied in practice). It would certainly put paid to a curriculum based upon community studies and the expressive arts.

Yet another solution to the dilemmas of examining at sixteen-plus is suggested by Daunt. As an alternative to examinations, pupils would be given 'a detailed and descriptive profile without grades, of their working qualities and achievements' (Daunt, 1975, p. 63). Such a profile would be nationally controlled, and pupils would have 'the right to enter for objective tests which would also be nationally controlled . . .' (Daunt, 1975, p. 63). Let us be clear what may be expected of such profiles. Instead of the limited claim, implicit in an examination certificate, to a moderate degree of knowledge or skill in some subject or discipline, the 'profile' will constitute a much fuller and richer description of the pupil in question. It is, perhaps, too early in the evolution of such profiles to know whether they will provide an adequate and ethically satisfactory substitute for conventional public examinations. To an extent, a 'character' reference is provided by most schools today for an employer, or university or college admissions officer. The 'profile' presumably goes very much further than this in its descriptiveness. One may be sceptical, however, that such profiles will contain any more than positive or noncommittal statements about the pupil. Yet, if it is a character description we want as employers, etc., we require it to include 'warts and all'. So far, according to a Schools Council report, only 25 schools from 96 English LEAs were using profiles. The report claims that teachers 'did not like being asked to assess personal qualities like honesty or initiative, often on slender, or non-existent evidence' (quoted in *The TES*, 19 January 1982, p. 10).

It seems that the creation of comprehensive schools has made for well-nigh insoluble dilemmas over curricula, their examination and assessment. At one extreme, there are those who urge the abandonment of any kind of formal assessment – pointing to its cost, the practical difficulties in its organisation, and its divisiveness in the comprehensive school. In the place of the CSE and the GCE, there would be substituted school based assessments of pupil performance – perhaps partly graded and partly 'profiled'. At the opposite extreme, there are some advocates of formal, objective tests for *all* pupils in comprehensive schools, externally marked according to national criteria. Such tests would distinguish between the different curricula followed by groups of pupils differentiated by ability and aptitude. Somewhere in the middle between these opposite and warring camps are those that believe a merger between the CSE and the GCE to create a common sixteen-plus examination, is the best way forward, despite the obvious administrative and political difficulties facing such a reform (first suggested by the now defunct Schools Council in 1970). But if such a reform is gradually accepted by the schools, will it end the divisiveness within comprehensive schools? I think not, as, firstly, children in the bottom 40 percentiles (40 per cent approximately of the schools' intake) will not be considered intellectually able enough to sit the new examinations. Thus there will continue to be a sharp and visible division between those pupils sitting public examinations and those not. And second, the exam papers themselves, it now seems fairly clear, in order to be acceptable to the putative examination boards, will distinguish between pupils who, following somewhat separate courses, will be separated into different teaching groups.

It is, of course, possible that the future of examinations at sixteen-plus will cease to be very much a matter of concern if pupils, *de facto* if not *de jure*, remain in some form of schooling until seventeen. This possibility, if fulfilled, will not, I suspect, relieve comprehensive schools of the dilemmas intrinsic to their organisation. As Auriol Stevens puts it: 'Comprehensives are living with an unresolved and possibly unresolvable conflict between egalitarianism and elitism.' (1980, p. 42.) Nevertheless the consequences of comprehensive reorganisation for pupils aged sixteen to eighteen is important, and will be considered in the next chapter – along with the notion of the 'comprehensive' university.

7 Comprehensive schooling: beyond sixteen

'It is not logical to suppose that the principles of comprehensive education can or should stop with the end of compulsory schooling.' Professor Robin Pedley, 1977.

The demise of the sixth form

Circular 10/65 recommended the all-through 11–18 school as 'in many respects the simplest and best solution' to the vexed problem of going comprehensive (para. 6). Such a school, necessarily, would include a sixth form. In contrast, the circular simply stated the advantages and limitations of a system of comprehensive schools with an age range of eleven to sixteen combined with a sixth-form college for pupils of sixteen and over. And whilst the circular recorded that the Secretary of State for Education (Crosland in 1965) believed 'the issues have been sufficiently debated to justify a limited number of experiments' with sixth-form colleges, such was the Secretary's caution that he hoped LEAs considering such experiments would 'consult with his Department at an early stage' (para. 20).

Support for sixth forms in comprehensive schools, and reserve concerning the value of sixth-form colleges as an alternative, is also expressed by other advocates of reorganisation. For example, Benn and Simon argue that to succumb to the 'temptation to remove sixth forms from existing comprehensive schools or to fail to agree to their being built up in certain areas, because present "numbers" do not immediately justify their provision would be short-sighted' (1970, p. 355). The existence of sixth forms in comprehensive schools was clearly vital to the claim that they were the equal of grammar schools, either now abolished or as yet living in uneasy coexistence. As Dennison points out: 'In many newly established comprehensive schools, the development of a prosperous sixth form, attracting at least as many

125

children, and achieving results comparable with the previous grammar school, was essential for the school to gain public confidence.' (1981, p. 142.) Newly established comprehensive schools were thus eager to extend or create their own sixth forms. Headmaster Maurice Holt, writing in 1978, noted that 'there are few 11–16 schools which would pass up the chance of their own sixth form if it were offered' (p. 148).

And yet in 1981, Fred Naylor, formerly sixth-form curriculum and examinations officer for the Schools Council, could aptly entitle a pamphlet of his published under the aegis of the Centre for Policy Studies: *Crisis in the Sixth Form.* The crisis to which his title draws attention is no less than the disappearance of sixth forms from our maintained schools. Like whales, sixth forms are an endangered species. Evidence of their decline is found in a review, *Education for 16–19 year Olds,* undertaken in 1980 for the government and local authority associations, by a group of administrators and teachers led by Neil Macfarlane, then a junior minister at the DES. One part of the evidence is the small size of many school sixth forms. As the Macfarlane review pointed out, 'in some 1,100 schools the number of pupils over the minimum school-leaving age was 50 or less in 1978–79' (p. 8). And whilst in some LEAs the sizes of sixth forms are small and diminishing, in other authorities school sixth forms have been abolished in favour of sixth-form or tertiary colleges. Indeed, Macfarlane notes that (1980, p. 8): 'Two out of every five 16–19 year olds receiving full-time or sandwich education are now taught in institutions catering solely for students of sixteen-plus.'

We may recall once again that, however misleadingly, comprehensive schools were advocated on the grounds that they would provide a grammar school education for all. Of such a grammar school education, that provided by its sixth form was reckoned to be the best part. The Spens Report on secondary education with special reference to grammar schools and technical high schools, had claimed that: 'There is general agreement that much of what is most valuable in the grammar school tradition depends on the existence of a sixth form.' (1938, p. xx.) In addition, comprehensive schools and their supporters wanted sixth forms for their schools. Why is it then, that so many of such schools have lost (or are losing) their sixth forms? And why is it likely that most state schools will see the last of their pupils at the age of sixteen?

The conventional and official explanation blames falling rolls for the demise of the sixth form. The Macfarlane review argues that the fall in the numbers of 16–19 year olds has led 'to small sixth forms becoming increasingly common in the late 1980s' and puts sixth forms in jeopardy (1980, p. 8). Macfarlane is surely right in arguing against maintaining small sixth forms. As Briault points out: 'rich sixth-form experiences depend a good deal on the academic and social peer groups being of adequate size' (1980, p. 238). If a school can provide opportunities to study only a limited number of 'A' levels, and those in groups of two or three pupils, this is 'a sorry contrast to the opportunities in a sixth-form college or a school sixth form of two hundred' (1980, p. 238). Indeed, Macfarlane goes so far as to argue that whilst '12–16 subjects [at 'A' level] is generally regarded as a reasonable range to be offered by a single institution such a range would almost inevitably exclude many "minority" subjects' (1980, p. 15).

Yet another difficulty with the small sixth form is that it drains away scarce teaching resources from the lower school attended by the majority of pupils. If a small sixth form can only be staffed by neglecting the lower school, the sixth form is difficult to justify. It is therefore interesting to note that the Spens Report decided not to support the replacement of the then selective (and divisive) system by multilateral (precursors to comprehensive) schools. Their grounds were that: 'a sixth form can only play its traditional part in the life of the school if it contains a reasonably high proportion of the pupils in the school. This could scarcely be the case if only half the pupils, or probably less, were on the grammar 'side' [of the then multilateral school] and were with comparatively few exceptions the only recruits for a sixth form' (1938, p. xx).

Nevertheless, if the Macfarlane group was correct in its judgement that small sixth forms are not feasible because they are uneconomic, make poor use of what specialist teachers are available, and fail to provide enough in the way of stimulus for the most able pupils, was the Macfarlane group right to blame falling rolls for the decline in the size of sixth forms? Naylor (1981) argues strongly to the contrary, citing demographic evidence which draws attention to differences between the fall in numbers amongst those that traditionally stay on at school and those that do not. As is now becoming clear, the decline in numbers of births is not uniform between all the population groups categorised by the Registrar General of births and deaths. Broadly speaking, the decline in numbers of children born to those classified by the Registrar General, on the basis of occupation, into social classes III, IV and V (skilled, semi-skilled, and unskilled manual labour respectively) has been relatively greater than the fall in numbers of those born to parents in social classes I (professional and managerial), II (intermediate), and those in non-manual occupations in social class III. As sociologists frequently point out and deplore, sixth forms recruit largely from children of parents in non-manual and skilled manual employment – the very groups whose numbers have fallen least in recent years. Further, as Naylor observes, the wave of children coming through the schools moved into the sixth forms at its peak in the late 1970s and early 1980s. Whatever the late 1980s will reveal, falling rolls will not explain the size of school sixth forms in the early 1980s.

It seems, therefore, unlikely that the numbers will fall of those wanting to stay on into what Macfarlane calls the 'traditional sixth form with its emphasis on A-level studies . . . [that] is essentially concerned with high academic standards of work and the personal growth of the pupil' (1980, p. 29). Indeed, their numbers are likely to be swollen by those repeating 'O' levels, and perhaps attempting some 'A' level work even if this is not seen as preparatory for university and college. However, it is equally clear that there is not a sufficient number of pupils, in each and every school designated comprehensive, to create a sixth form of such a size to make sixth-form study a feasible proposition. Given the haphazard patchwork of comprehensive reorganisation, as detailed in previous chapters, this is scarcely surprising. As was pointed out repeatedly by experienced teachers and administrators, only in favourable circumstances will an eight-form comprehensive school develop such a sixth form. Indeed, Naylor (1981) suggests that a fifteen-form entry school is necessary for a sixth form that will match up to the standards of sixth-form organisation recommended in the Macfarlane review. Such schools are the exception rather than the rule. The average size of a comprehensive school is somewhat under 1,000 pupils, and will probably fall further under the impact of falling rolls, despite the desperate efforts of educational administrators to close schools and rationalise resources.

Comprehensive reorganisation has thus created in many LEAs two types of schools: 11–16 schools often based upon former secondary moderns, located in the 'inner-city', and struggling to create or sustain their sixth forms; and 11–18 schools, often to be found in the suburbs, based upon former grammar schools, and maintaining their sixth-form numbers – indeed, these are perhaps augmented by 'new sixth-formers' repeating 'O' level courses, or pursuing some relatively new courses other than 'A' levels. The inevitable consequence is that 'Schools which retain sixth forms tend to have more prestige in the eyes of many parents and are apt to be the most popular first choice for pupils at eleven or twelve. The residual schools then suffer both from failing to attract a due proportion of the most able pupils, as well as in limitations of staffing that go with both a smaller school and the absence of advanced work.' (Macfarlane, 1980, p. 30.)

Naylor argues that the proliferation of small comprehensive schools, not the decline in pupil numbers, is the root cause of the 'crisis in the sixth form'. If there is truth in his argument then the reorganisation of secondary education on comprehensive lines has had consequences contrary to those hoped for and predicted by its supporters. The advocates of comprehensive schooling wanted sixth forms for such schools – however many virtues are now discovered in sixth-form and tertiary colleges.

The LEAs, in response to the crisis of the sixth form, are busily re-reorganising their secondary schools: an upheaval that Professor Pedley, suggests 'cannot be contemplated, although some modifications are clearly possible' (1977, p. 36). Rather more than modifications are proposed in the Macfarlane review: 'The overwhelming majority of authorities must, we believe, urgently consider the institutional base of their provision.' (1980, p. 12.)

Many LEAs are, indeed, faced with an unpalatable choice between abolishing all their schools' sixth forms, or maintaining some schools with sixth forms in coexistence with 11–16 schools. Either solution has its disadvantages and courts political unpopularity. Much depends upon the political party in power (however temporarily) at town or county hall. For example, Birmingham, in June 1982, under a new Conservative administration, overturned a Labour plan to abolish sixth forms and replace them with 'open access colleges'. Instead, the new administration intends to retain sixth forms in 22 of its secondary schools and close 21 other schools. Such a proposal is, fairly predictably, open to the accusation that it will 'bring back a system of secondary modern and grammar schools by the back door' (statement by the teachers' unions reported in *The TES*, 25 June 1982).

There is little doubt that LEAs face considerable problems over this issue. It is now quite clear that all schools labelled 'comprehensive' cannot maintain sixth forms; many of the schools are far too small and lack the specialist teaching staff necessary. Yet to maintain some schools with sixth forms whilst most do not strengthens the already marked inequalities between comprehensive schools, as the Macfarlane review was quick to note (see above). Thus, if all schools cannot have sixth forms none shall, is the logic of the comprehensive principle. Comprehensive school supporters are thus driven, contrary to their earlier expressed convictions ('to remove sixth forms from comprehensive schools . . . would be short-sighted') to campaign forcefully for both the abolition of all schools' sixth forms and for the establishment of sixth-form and tertiary colleges.

And yet are these alternatives to schools' sixth forms much in keeping with the comprehensive principle either? The very first sixth-form college was proposed for Croydon by its then Chief Education Officer. Pedley notes: 'His scheme was presented as a means of making academic education more efficient, not of facilitating a change to comprehensive education.' (1977, p. 22.) Sixth-form colleges offer one- or two-year courses leading to 'O' and 'A' levels. They are thus very much concerned with examination success – one wonders how easily this fits in with some views of comprehensive education. Of course, many sixth-form colleges encourage non-examination studies, and may increasingly have students who are not strong examination candidates. Nevertheless, the emphasis on exams is there – as it is amongst the staff, many of whom may find the sixth-form college a quiet haven in comparison to the hustle and bustle of many comprehensive schools. Indeed, the necessity for such schools to recruit specialist staff (mainly honours graduates) may mean that sixth-form colleges have (and will) become attractive to teachers who formerly would have taught in the grammar schools.

Critics of sixth-form colleges draw attention to the shortness of the courses to be found within them – one or two years in length. As the Macfarlane review points out, 'The teachers have to make special efforts to get to know students, many of whom leave after one year.' (1981, p. 30.) In contrast, Pedley suggests that a school's sixth form 'has the immense advantage of a continuous relationship with teachers who have seen its students grow to this point, who know their strengths and weaknesses, their potential and what is needed to develop it in each individual' (1978, p. 90).

Indeed, some supporters of comprehensive schooling are sceptical of the virtue of the sixth-form college – for they fear that such a college might prove a defensible redoubt for supporters of the grammar school. The Crowther Report (1959) on the education of boys and girls between the ages of fifteen and eighteen, commended the grammar school sixth form as providing a 'close link with the university, specialisation, independent work, intellectual disciplineship and social responsibility' (para. 337). Yet Crowther was moved to ask: 'Is a sixth form in this sense to be regarded as a luxury of the past, as a privelege which cannot extend beyond the leading schools, something which cannot be generalised?' (para. 337.) 'Yes' is the affirmitive answer to this question from some supporters of comprehensive reorganisation; and the sixth-form college is not to be welcomed for that reason. The preferred alternative is the tertiary college.

This curiously named college is the local 'tech' written a little larger. Technical colleges, of course, fulfil a whole range of useful functions for the communities they serve. They provide full-time and part-time training courses with a strong vocational bias. In addition, they may be centres for adult education and leisure activities from flower arranging to contemporary dance. They also provide opportunities to school leavers and mature students for 'O' and 'A' level work – thus providing a most useful 'second chance' to take or re-take qualifications useful for employment, and college and university entry. However, whilst providing a range of courses, shorter or longer, full-time and part-time, vocational, cultural, or 'leisure' in character, the colleges may have very little in the way of a central core or focus. Indeed, Pedley remarks that in the technical college 'There is little community spirit comparable to that of a school – for example, the interest and participation in college teams and societies is low.' (1977, p. 18.) The question can then be put: 'Are such colleges suitable as the main institution for the education of the majority of our boys and girls who wish to stop in full-time education beyond the age of sixteen?'

It is sometimes argued that most boys and girls have had enough of school at sixteen; and even that minority, who see sixth-form work as a preparation for university or college, wish to break at sixteen with their school, and to start afresh at an institution specially established for 16–19 year olds. If there is truth in this, then the eagerness of pupils to leave school at sixteen is both cause and effect of the very difficulties comprehensive schools have in both creating and maintaining sixth forms. It is often argued by the supporters of sixth-form and tertiary colleges that their students prefer the relaxed and 'adult-like' atmosphere of the colleges to the (presumably) more restricted and 'child-like' ambience of the comprehensive school.

One suspects that a good deal of the prevailing interest in transforming local 'techs' into tertiary colleges arises largely from expediency. Most LEAs have such colleges sited fairly centrally. With some enlargement they can extend the 'O' and 'A' level courses they already provide to a wider range of pupils. And happily enough, the notion of bringing together students following a variety of courses in one institution can be given some social or educational justification, as in Shirley Williams's argument that 'The opportunities for students to mix socially and in extra-curricular activities make traditional distinctions between vocational and academic seem absurd; each group learns something about the work of the other.' (1981, p. 167.) It is interesting to note that Williams's argument assumes that she finds seemingly absurd the distinction between academic and vocational groups.

Segregation will be replaced by integration in social and extra-curricular activities – if, contrary to Pedley (see above), there are any such activities in the tertiary college.

What much of this argument about integration largely ignores are the difficulties facing colleges attempting to provide for many different types of students following diverse courses. Much criticism of comprehensive schooling focuses on just this problem: of adequately coping with the diverse needs and interests of children differing widely in ability and aptitude. Will tertiary colleges cope any better? Will distinctions between students following different courses give rise to differential claims on the resources of the colleges? Whatever the answers to these questions, pious talk about the virtues of (a perhaps largely unwanted) social integration will not suffice.

And what are the consequences for secondary schools that have their sixth forms abolished? It is difficult to believe that such abolition will be welcomed by the staff of comprehensive schools – however much they accept the comprehensive principle. As Dennison writes, for many teachers 'possession of a sixth form is vital, both to offer the intangible benefits of work satisfaction and high status to at least some staff and extra advancement possibilities to all' (1981, p. 144). Such teachers may now look elsewhere – to the sixth-form and tertiary college – for employment, thus depriving the 11–16 school of specialist staffing. The Macfarlane group indeed claim: 'There are indications from HMIs' surveys that, in a period of contracting population, financial constraint and known shortages of key specialist teachers, 11– or 12–16 schools are tending to experience more acutely than 11– or 12–18 schools, problems in achieving adequate curricular coverage and specialist staffing.' (1981, p. 31.) Many LEAs now operate a 'ring-fence' system by which they restrict appointments within their authority largely to teachers already in their employment. Such authorities when creating sixth-form colleges will, no doubt, in the first instance, offer appointments to teachers in schools closed down, or reduced to 11–16 schools. The teachers appointed may tend to be the most academically specialist, thus depriving the feeder schools of their services. Of course, parents and the general public may be told that close co-operation and co-ordination, between a variety of feeder schools and the sixth-form colleges, will readily overcome difficulties arising from discontinuities between schools and colleges of varying sizes and academic organisation. Such assurances, one suspects, will be viewed sceptically. 11–16 schools, deprived of specialist staff, will have to both limit their curricular offerings, and offer less in the way of higher level teaching for the more intellectually able children. This may well, ultimately, have its consequence for sixth-form colleges. Minority subjects will suffer: if, for example, Latin is not taught in the lower or feeder school, pupils will be that much less prepared for classical studies in the sixth-form college. Maths and science may also be the victims of the abolition of schools' sixth forms. It still remains difficult to recruit specialist teachers for science and maths – even for schools with thriving sixth forms. Such teachers may well be reluctant to work in schools with no opportunities for sixth-form work, and where they will be expected to teach general science or maths throughout the school to every level of ability.

Discussion of appropriate ways of training and educating 16–19 year old boys and girls is obfuscated by youth unemployment. Schools and colleges come to be seen more and more as custodial institutions – keeping youth off the streets, and in addition, helping to reduce the statistic of unemployment. Boys and girls are better off in schools and colleges than in aimlessly roaming the streets and shopping centres. Yet many of them may learn more of value at work than in school; certainly, this is a view held by many youngsters. It is a curious aspect of the 'life-skill' courses, now provided for many unemployed boys and girls, that they seem intended to teach simple literacy and numeracy that, it might be thought, was the task of the schools to develop. Yet much contemporary thinking on the education and training of 16–19 year olds now seems to be based upon the pessimistic assumption that large-scale youth unemployment is here to stay. Perhaps it is; yet whether it is therefore sensible to put all 16–19 year olds in one type of college seems doubtful, given the failure of comprehensive schools to provide adequately for their varied intakes.

This section concludes my discussion of the impact of comprehensive reorganisation on secondary schools. I intend to bring this chapter to its close with some consideration of the influence of comprehensive schooling on the educational attainments ('outcome' in more fashionable jargon) of its pupils. However, because supporters of comprehensive reorganisation have something to say about higher education, perhaps here – following on from my discussion of the sixth form – is the best place for discussion of the notion of the comprehensive university.

The comprehensive university

Leonard M. Cantor and I. F. Roberts, in their authoritative, *Further Education Today: A Critical Review*, dismiss as romantic Professor Pedley's advocacy of 'comprehensive universities embracing the whole range of post-18 provision' (1979, p. 197). But before we join in, and then pass on from this casual dismissal, let us consider how the view that grammar schools embrace the whole range of schooling for boys and girls aged eleven to eighteen might have appeared to (say) Ellen Wilkinson or George Tomlinson – Ministers of Education under Attlee in the Labour post-war administration. No doubt such suggestions were similarly casually dismissed This does suggest that we have to consider Pedley's suggestion with the seriousness it perhaps deserves.

In *Towards the Comprehensive University*, Pedley argues plausibly enough: 'It is not logical to suppose that the principles of comprehensive education can or should stop with the end of compulsory schooling.' (1977, p. 33.) Our doubts might be that such principles can be clearly stated; or if so stated, whether they would meet with much support. Nevertheless this statement is in the way of a warning shot across the bows – to remind us that no institution is sacrosanct, least of all the university. Whatever else universities are, they are intended to be places for the teaching of and research in a variety of intellectual disciplines. Furthermore – at least ideally – such places are open to all who can profit from them. Indeed, the Universal Declaration of Human Rights goes so far as to establish merit as the entry criterion for a higher education, for whereas 'Technical and professional education shall be generally available', 'higher education shall be equally accessible to all on the basis of merit' (Article 26 (1)).

Pedley, perhaps with these considerations in mind, asks the question '. . . does the word 'comprehensive' imply that entry to any course offered by the university is open to all regardless of whether they do or do not possess evidence that they are likely to profit from that course?' (1977, p. 89.) Pedley fails to answer his own semantic enquiry – perhaps because it might have established that a comprehensive university is a contradiction in terms. No doubt, Britain's Open University comes closest to Pedley's ideal of the comprehensive university. No formal educational qualifications are demanded of applicants; indeed such qualifications have at times been something of a disqualification for entry. Yet Naomi McIntosh, Head of the OU's Survey Research Department, in an article, 'The OU Student', notes that amongst those students dropping out before final registration (never mind graduation): 'the groups with no formal qualifications, or less than five 'O' levels, were the most vulnerable. This was particularly marked in science and maths.' (1974, p. 58.)

Pedley rightly hesitates to demand that universities teach everybody who wishes to enrol – irrespective of ability or any evidence of initial preparation for exacting university studies. More reasonably, he argues that 'what is required of a comprehensive institution of adult education is sufficient breadth and variety of study opportunities to satisfy the needs of all comers whether they be brilliant philosophers or illiterates' (1977, p. 89). No exception can be taken to this – at least in general terms – so long as what is understood as 'a comprehensive institution of adult education' is not a single university or college attempting to cope with the 'needs of all comers'. Indeed, one suspects that Pedley's vision of 'what is required' is already in sight in the shape of our further education colleges: 'This bewildering range of institutions comprises a very flexible system whose chief glory is, perhaps, that it provides an opportunity for everyone, whatever his or her capabilities in whatever time may be available, to follow a course of education or training.' (Cantor and Roberts, 1979, p. 195.) Such a system of colleges, plus polytechnics and universities, provide an abundance of provision for higher education in Britain.

It is difficult to avoid the impression that it is universities that are being lined up – like the maintained grammar schools – for destruction. In the face of the fact that Britain has varied provision in higher and further education, what other conclusion can be drawn? It is not the absence of educational provision but the unwillingness of many young people (and their employers) to make use of what is readily available which is the crux of the problem. The difficulties facing many polytechnics (and some universities) arise from their problems in recruiting students – not the absence of resources for teaching them. In these circumstances, universities with some small degree of autonomy, and recruiting the most intellectually able, become targets for the egalitarian minded.

Pedley, for example, attacks the 'binary principle' enunciated by Crosland when in office. Not so much from principle but rather more from expediency, the DES established (or permitted to come into being) two largely separate types of degree-awarding institutions: the universities, much expanded in the 1960s; and the polytechnics, developed in the late 1960s and early 1970s, and under the control of the LEAs. The 'binary principle', although established by a Labour Secretary of State for Education, could as readily justify separate schooling for children of differing ability and aptitude. Pedley quotes Crosland as saying 'at a time of rapid expansion and changing ideas we want not a monopoly position in higher education, but a variety of institutions under different control' (in Pedley 1977, p. 51). Despite, or because of, the good sense and liberality of this statement, Pedley is moved to say: 'Precisely the same argument can, with equal validity, or lack of it, be applied to the schools.' (1977, p. 51.)

In contradiction to Crosland's plea for a pluralist approach to higher education, Pedley urges: 'In a truly democratic society the resources of the university, so long reserved for an elite minority, must be thrown open to all . . .' (1977, p. 3). It is certainly true that only a minority of 16–19 year olds attend universities in Britain; whether they therefore constitute an elite minority, in any meaningful sense of that much abused word, may be doubted. It is also difficult to see what is meant by 'open to all'. All that are suitably qualified? Yet Pedley has (see above) refused to give an unequivocally affirmative answer to his own question as to whether a 'comprehensive' university 'is open to all regardless of whether they do or do not possess evidence that they are likely to profit from that course'. In what Pedley describes as 'a comprehensive, post-school organisation', 'selection would increasingly be self-selection, made under guidance from teachers and counsellors' (1977, p. 52). What a remarkably paternalistic world this conjures up whereby open competition for scarce resources (to employ Flew's redescription of equality of opportunity) is replaced by 'self-selection' made under guidance from teachers and counsellors.

In some passages, Pedley's comments on universities are distinctly populist in character. He refers to: 'mounting criticism of the privileged position which universities seemed to occupy in the national life, and what were seen as the abuses of that privilege' (1977, p. 45). Professor Pedley points out, chillingly, 'the independence of professors can run counter to the national interest. . . .' 'And even if the universities are found not guilty on all counts the principle that a national system of education, at whatever level, should in the last resort be controlled by representatives of the people is likely to be upheld by a majority outside the universities and by a minority within them.' (1977, p. 46.) The latter statement is clearly a *non sequitor*. No one disputes that *in the last resort* a national (or state) system of education must be controlled by representatives of the people. That is indeed why we have a parliament and an elected government. What is in dispute is the degree of freedom permitted to educational institutions in the last resort controlled by our elected representatives. Judging by Pedley's comments on the dangers of permitting a degree of independence to the professoriate (harmful to the national interest – but defined by whom?), the conclusion must be: not a great deal.

Pedley's more detailed proposal is for 'some 100 comprehensive universities in England and Wales in place of the present unplanned assortment of 34 universities, 30 polytechnics and 44 colleges or institutes of education or higher education' (1977, p. 86). Such 'universities' would draw their students from the regions in which they are located. Oxford comprehensive university would presumably recruit from Oxfordshire; whilst Bradford would draw from Bradford and West Yorkshire, along catchment area lines drawn carefully to avoid competition with Leeds and Salford comprehensive universities. Such comprehensive post-school organisations would be under the control of regional representatives of the people, yet 'no one group or body would or should be in control; comprehensive adult education must be a co-operative enterprise if such essentials as freedom of speech, the advancement of knowledge, the efficient use of resources and the enlargement of educational opportunity are to be preserved or achieved' (Pedley, 1977, p. 91). One wonders how many of the 'essentials' listed above would long be preserved in a system of regional control in which 'no one group or body would or should be in control' – or how long that anarchic state of affairs would last, and who would finally emerge as the regional controllers.

Yet Pete Ashby, a former full-time deputy president of the National Union of Students, in a contribution to a collection of essays, *Equality and Education* (1980), argues that Pedley's proposals do not go far enough in pursuit of educational equality. Ashby writes that Pedley's 'concept of the comprehensive institution is both ill-conceived and misleading: ill-conceived because an institution-centred model is too restricted to meet the full variety of needs, and misleading because it implies that with a few more mergers and regrouping into "super universities" the new comprehensive era will be here' (1980, p. 309). Ashby does share Pedley's distrust of universities as they are now, and he argues that concepts such as 'impartiality', 'excellence' and 'scholarship' are used by the universities in a plot to 'exclude the vast majority of the population . . .' (1980, p. 304). Ashby proposes that 'universities should be brought under LEA control and LEAs made responsible for unified planning of all post-school education' (p. 310).

The notion of universities being placed in the hands of the LEAs is favoured by egalitarian reformers of higher education. It is urged on two grounds: first, that it is more democratic; and second, that it would permit more efficient and unified control over higher education. Both these grounds may be questioned. LEA control is not likely to be more democratic than the present parliamentary and DES supervision of universities as national institutions. The way in which LEAs 'democratically' established comprehensive schooling (see chapter 3) is strong evidence for that. The fact that relationships are strained between many LEAs and their polytechnics suggest LEAs do have difficulty in running institutions of higher education, which may be regional if not national in character. In addition, as LEA control over secondary schools has produced no efficient and unitary system, one may beg leave to doubt whether extending LEA control to cover universities will help create such unity in higher education.

Advocates of increasing educational provision never consider the vexed question of resources – except to demand more. Ashby quite rightly points out that '. . . a mass system [of full-time education] could only be brought about through a major injection of public resources into post-school education' (1980, p. 306). This conclusion is echoed by a fellow contributor to *Education and Equality*, Les Brook, who points out: 'Our concept of provision for the 16–19 implies massive capital investment in education.' (p. 285.)

Yet when we look for the justification of such a 'massive capital investment', it is not to be found. It is taken for granted that more education for the 16–19 year olds is so self-evidently good that no one but an unreformed and unrepentant Scrooge could question the apportionment of public funds to it. On what grounds, however, can we justify 'a major injection of public resources' – given the finite character of such resources – for the 16–19 year olds at the expense (say) of the health service, or the care of the elderly? Our prisons are a disgrace to a civilised nation. Why should we not direct some of our necessarily limited public resources to their improvement? And within education, primary schooling, relative to secondary and further, has not been so well financed or supported. Why should we improve services for the 16–19 year olds at the expense (one suspects) of the 6–9 year olds? The assumption is that resources are infinite, and it is only a matter of political will to direct them in the approved and desired direction.

It is, however, fair to say that the abolition of the universities, and the creation in their place of comprehensive, post-school organisations, is not yet high on any political party's agenda. Nevertheless, the history of the reorganisation of secondary education may have at least one lesson: that valued institutions can be destroyed – despite there existing no widespread support for their destruction, and contrary to the expressed opinions of most parents and teachers. Let us, then, not forget Pedley's warning that there is no logic in supposing comprehensive education can or should stop at the end of compulsory schooling.

The evaluation of comprehensive schooling

Shirley Williams believes that 'The only conceivable argument against comprehensive education is the educational one, that children's academic achievements will be less good if they are educated together rather than being segregated according to their abilities.' (1981, p. 156.) So whatever else comprehensive schooling may fail to do, if the pupils' academic achievements are at least as good (but no better) than they might have been in the selective system, all is well. Although it is gratifying to note the emphasis here on academic attainment, and the recognition of the importance of education for schooling – nevertheless this is indeed the most minimal expectation of comprehensive schooling. For Jane Steedman, in the concluding remarks to her lengthy report, *Progress in Secondary Schools* points out: 'It may be that parents expected more, during this period of reorganisation of secondary schooling [covered in the report], from schools called 'comprehensives' than from secondary moderns.' (1980, p. 231.) Yes, for after all the purpose of going comprehensive – with all the upheaval and distress it caused – was surely to make things better. As Steedman puts it: 'Parents would believe, perhaps, that reorganisation was intended to improve schooling.' (1980, p. 231.) Williams's requirement that comprehensive schools are justified if they show themselves to be no worse than the schools they replaced is not enough; comprehensive schools must be shown to be better than the schools they replaced if reorganisation is to be judged a success. What is the evidence?

Perhaps in the nature of things such evidence is both hard to come by *and* to evaluate. As supporters of comprehensive reorganisation are swift to point out, it is difficult to make a comparative study of selective and non-selective systems of education; to judge comprehensive schools relative to selective schools is not always fair. As Caroline Benn has noted, the existence of grammar schools may make it difficult for comprehensive schools to enrol the most intellectually able children. In those circumstances, any comparison between the two systems is not comparing like with like. For we are comparing one system of schooling, in which the distribution of intellectual ability is skewed in favour of the most intellectually capable, with another in which the bias is towards the least intellectually able. Thus our conclusions about the relative success of the two systems must be weighted to allow for differences in measured intelligence, aptitude and ability in their two populations. What further complicates the matter is that the causes (other than schooling) of differences in academic achievement are not fully understood, and are the subject of much controversy: as between those who place stress on inherited ability, and those who consider home background and social class to be the most important in influencing educational attainment.

Nor is there full agreement about the standards on which the two systems are to be judged. Within the selective system, the success of grammar schools was measured in a different way to that of secondary modern schools. The supporters of comprehensive schools argued that these schools should be judged in yet another way – with less stress on examination results, and more on such aspects of school life as fraternity and social integration. Some of the more extreme supporters of comprehensive schooling have argued for radical reforms of the curriculum. The subject-based curriculum must go – to be replaced by 'integrated studies' in which boundaries between academic, vocational, and practical work would be destroyed. Indeed, some sociologists of education have argued (and deplored) that much of what is taught in schools 'is dominated by academic curricula with a rigid stratification [sic] knowledge' (Young, 1971, p. 36). Strong differences of view on how the success of comprehensives ought to be measured obviously make for great difficulties in comparing such schools with those they replaced.

Most of the problems involved in comparing selective and non-selective systems were encountered by the researchers working for the National Child Development Study (NCDS). I have referred to this study above and in chapter 3; its research report *Progress in Secondary Schools* provides at least some evidence on the success or failure of comprehensive schooling. As I noted in chapter 3, the report is of a research project which had 'its origins in a much longer term study of all the people in Great Britain born in one week of March, 1958' (1980, p. 1). The report, funded by the DES, attempts to evaluate 'aspects of progress in selective and non-selective schools'.

The NCDS is an example of a longitudinal social survey. The progress of a sample of children ('cohort' in research language) is monitored and measured from their birth to maturity and beyond. Dr J. W. B. Douglas, himself a director of a well-known longitudinal survey, has argued that: 'cohort studies provide the most efficient and also the cheapest opportunity to assess the effectiveness of new services and new policies' (1976, p. 20). Douglas specifically drew attention to the reorganisation of secondary education, and asked: 'In secondary education, has the introduction of the comprehensive system been associated with greater social equality in achievement and a breaking down of social barriers in the community, and if so have the greatest changes occurred in those local education areas which have been most thorough in reorganising the schools, and is it most clearly seen among individuals who have enjoyed a comprehensive education?' (p. 19.) Douglas claims that: 'These are all questions that can be answered if we are in a position to compare national cohorts appropriately situated in time.' (p. 20).

Nevertheless, Jane Steedman draws attention to methodological problems facing the researchers: for example information from the NCDS was 'not expressly designed for the purpose' of evaluating 'aspects of progress in selective and non-selective schools'. In addition, the cohort was passing through secondary schools between 1969 and 1974 – described by Steedman as 'a very particular period in the piecemeal and lengthy progress of comprehensive reorganisation' (p. 2). There were difficulties in comparing schools as the NCDS is 'child-based' rather than 'school-based'. Many children in the cohort are excluded for consideration in Steedman's report. Children attending direct grant and independent schools were omitted, as were children about whom there was no information on parental occupation. Many others were removed from the sample because they changed from one school to another. The final sample was divided between grammar, secondary modern, and comprehensive schools.

The children in the sample had been tested in a variety of ways at ages eleven and sixteen. The tests included: a reading test, a maths test, a self-rated performance test at English, and maths; liking for school (pupils' views on 'I don't like school'); school behaviour ratings by teachers, and by parents. In addition, proportions were estimated of those children: wanting professional, manual, or clerical work for first job; considering 'being well paid' and 'opportunity of helping others' as important in a job; and of parents 'satisfied' with their children's education in their present school.

Steedman points out that a simple comparison of the test scores of children at the three types of schools would be misleading. She argues it is wrong to believe that all differences between test scores at eleven and test scores at sixteen are attributable to schooling. For example, some of the differences may relate to family background and social class origins. The 'raw scores' were adjusted to take into account: social class (as measured by occupation of parent); parental interest; differences between boys and girls; differences between school at eleven, or age twelve or thirteen; 'and sometimes . . . other factors', not named (p. 201). 'The investigation . . . was therefore not an examination of absolute levels of attainment, or other aspects of sixteen year olds but was designed to ascertain, as far as attainments went, at least, the relative progress of those in different kinds of schools – that is, the amount by which they had advanced beyond the stage reached by eleven years old.' (Steedman, 1980, p. 207.)

What conclusions does this research project reach? In the journal of the National Children's Bureau, *Concern*, the findings are summarised in these terms: 'Those in comprehensive schools did as well and as badly as if selection had still operated and some had gone to grammars and the rest to secondary moderns.' (1980, p. 32.) In other words, if this statement does indeed broadly summarise the findings of the research project, comprehensive reorganisation had not improved levels of attainment at all. Yet despite Steedman's comment that 'this research cannot give an answer to whether one system is better for children in general' (1980, p. 227), Shirley Williams, for one, claimed there was evidence enough in the report to refute arguments that comprehensive reorganisation was no improvement on the selective system of education.

However, this summary of the NCDS project has been criticised for its presentation and interpretation of its own findings. Caroline Cox and John Marks in an appraisal of *Progress in Secondary Schools* argued that the data had been 'doctored'. In *Real Concern* (1981) they drew attention to a number of features of the report that in their opinion were examples of 'doctoring' and a misleading presentation of the findings. They picked out the fact that details were not provided of the 'raw data', that is the test scores at eleven and sixteen before adjustments for any background factors. Cox and Mark also claimed the reading test was inadequate for the width of ability tested: it did not sufficiently distinguish between the least and the most capable readers, and by conflating test scores might thereby give a misleading picture of progress in reading, or lack of it.

Certainly the degree to which allowances should be made for background factors does present a problem. One can understand and sympathise with the researchers' view that weighting was required to adjust for factors that might influence test scores other than schooling. Nevertheless, there is a danger here, as overweighting such scores would eliminate any possibility of determining the influence of school. Steedman writes: '. . . in an analysis *where background factors are allowed for*, the maths test performance of comprehensive pupils who were among the top attainers at eleven suggests that, by sixteen, they had made as much progress in mathematics as the equivalent grammar school pupils . . .' (1980, p. 111, my italics). Cox and Marks state that they have a 'real concern' that not only is information on raw data missing, but that provided on the weight given to background factors is inadequate.

Cox and Marks, in addition, claimed that the research findings are presented in such a way that any result favourable to comprehensive schooling is highlighted, whilst evidence unfavourable is either minimised or explained away. I have given an example of this in chapter 3: that of criticism by parents of comprehensive schools, justified as showing 'a certain criticality [sic] or involvement in decisions about schooling among parents which some schools would hope to foster' (Steedman, 1980, p. 207). Cox and Marks also question the omission of children from direct grant and independent schools from the sample. Such an omission, they argue, lessens the comparative value of the findings of the report.

There is a curious sequel to *Real Concern*; the British Educational Research Association (BERA) took the unusual step of publishing an open letter announcing that the executive council of BERA is 'deeply concerned' at the methods employed by Cox and Marks in their pamphlet. The BERA executive, in particular, took exception to the accusation by Cox and Marks that the NCDS researchers had 'doctored' their evidence and were 'excessively partisan' in their interpretation and presentation. What 'equally concerned' the executive was that *Real Concern* was published under the aegis of the Centre for Policy Studies, understood to be politically close to the Conservative Party, and yet 'given the standing of objective educational research institutions' by the press. Whether the pamphleteering of the Centre is, indeed, given this standing is a moot point, but it is interesting to note that the chairman of the advisory group to the project that led to *Progress in Secondary Schools* was Professor A. H. Halsey – an adviser to the Labour Secretary of State for Education, 1965–68, and one who has never disguised his belief in socialism, egalitarianism, and comprehensive schooling.[13]

Viewed in a way most favourable to comprehensive schooling, *Progress in Secondary Schools*, provides evidence only that children did just about as well academically in 1974 in comprehensive schools as in grammar and secondary moderns. However, the report also provides evidence that parental dissatisfaction was greatest with comprehensive schools, and that truancy and poor behaviour was more likely to be found in comprehensives than in grammar and secondary modern schools. The achievements of comprehensive schools begin to look remarkably slight, although we must bear in mind that – as ever – even the tentative and guarded conclusions of the report are qualified by the much repeated warning that few of the comprehensive schools in the sample were as yet truly comprehensive in character.

Another way of judging the success or failure of comprehensive schooling is by comparing GCE 'O' and 'A' level results before and after comprehensive reorganisation. During the 1950s and 1960s more and more boys and girls were stopping on after the compulsory school-leaving age and gaining more passes at 'O' and 'A' level. For example, in 1960–61, 8.3 per cent of the age group gained one or more 'A' levels, whilst in 1970–71 the percentage had increased to 15.5. But after reaching a peak of 15.7 in 1972–73, it has remained at about 15 per cent ever since – despite the raising of the school leaving age to sixteen in 1973, largely justified in terms of increasing opportunities. There is, also, evidence that the proportion of university entrants from manual and clerical backgrounds declined throughout the 1970s.

If we look at 'O' level results for England and Wales at the beginning and end of the 1970s, the percentage of school leavers with at least one 'O' level pass did increase from 1970–71 to 1979–80; from slightly over 40 per cent to a little under 50 per cent for boys and from over 40 per cent to about 55 per cent for girls. So far so good – yet when we look at combinations of English and maths with science and modern languages, the picture changes.[14] In these combinations of subjects, the achievement of girls between the beginning and the end of the decade increased only marginally, whilst with boys the percentage has fallen. The decline in 'O' level achievement is most marked in the case of modern languages which has declined in percentage terms for both the sexes, but more greatly with boys. And yet this was during a period that according to the HMIs' survey (1979) there was, if anything, too much stress on the importance of preparation for 'O' level examinations in comprehensive schools.

When Dr Rhodes Boyson, employing figures similar to those above, argued in a speech to the National Council for Educational Standards (June 1982) that comprehensive schooling was responsible for the failure to raise GCE results, the response was fairly predictable. Joan Sallis, for example, a spokesperson for CASE, argued that it was 'absurd to judge schools by 'A' levels or the proportion of a particular class that get into higher education' (quoted in *The TES*, 30 April 1982).[15] No doubt, it is partial to judge schools *only* by 'A' level results, and by their success in increasing their numbers of university entrants. Yet the capacity of comprehensive schools to improve the educational attainments of their most intellectually able pupils is surely a matter of concern to members of CASE. Indeed, there may well be a link between academic success in schools and other forms of achievement. This seems to be the conclusion of Professor Rutter, and his team of researchers, in their survey of London schools, in which they observe: 'Schools with good academic achievements tended to be more successful in maintaining good attendance and behaviour.' (1979, p. 198.)

Of course, it is quite mistaken to claim that the failure of secondary schools to maintain the increase in 'O' and 'A' level passes that was a feature of the 1950s and the 1960s, was – without dispute – caused by comprehensive reorganisation. There are, no doubt, other factors in the social, economic and political life of British society that might equally be suggested as the culprits. That comprehensive reorganisation slowed down – and some instances reversed – the improvement in academic attainments remains, then, simply an hypothesis. But this can give no comfort to the supporters of a reorganisation of secondary schooling so constantly and insistently promoted on the grounds that such a reorganisation would provide greater opportunities for one and all. It certainly will not do to argue, in both explanation and justification of the failure of comprehensive schooling to raise educational standards, that such standards are manifestations of middle-class values within the schools, and must be rejected as such. For as Gerald Grace, in a study of teaching in the ILEA, points out, 'important sections of this population [parents in the ILEA] want "discipline" for their children, support unliberated concepts, such as school uniform and single-sex schools, expect to see visible and early signs of achievement in basic competencies, and want their children to "get on" within the existing social and economic order' (1978, p. 62).

8 Conclusion

'To dream the impossible dream', from *The Man from La Mancha*, Joe Darian, 1968.

The failure of comprehensive schooling

In the early days of comprehensive schooling, its introduction was often described as an 'experiment'. For instance, C. A. R. Crosland in 1956 suggested a future Labour government should encourage LEAs 'to be more audacious in experimenting with comprehensive schools in the light of the marked success . . . of the experiments to date' (1956, p. 275). It may well be that the word, 'experiments', used here, is no more than a rhetorical device: not to be taken seriously or literally, but rather employed to lull opponents into believing that there still remains the possibility of an abandonment of comprehensive reorganisation if the 'experiments' fail. If, however, the supporters of comprehensive schooling genuinely believe it to be experimental, they must face up to the possibility that the experiments will reveal that such schooling fails. Indeed, the purpose of experiments is to test theories and principles as rigorously as possible; and the history of experimental science shows that few theories and principles ultimately survive that rigorous testing which aims to discover not confirmatory but counter-evidence.

Have, then, comprehensive schools failed in practice – thus demonstrating the inadequacy of the comprehensive theory or principle? It is important to note that questions of failure and success must be considered relative to the theory in question. Thus comprehensive schools must be tested relative to their own theory or principle – no mean task given the lack of any clear and authoritative expression of this theory. In so far as such a theory be construed from the writings of the supporters of comprehensive schooling, I have contrasted that theory with the facts of reorganisation, both without and within the schools. What follows in this chapter summarises my findings on the success or

146

failure of comprehensive schooling – although I am aware that to describe comprehensive reorganisation as an experiment may be no more than analogical; and I have considerable doubts about the coherence of the comprehensive theory or principle itself.

It is my view that in Britain comprehensive schooling has failed in practice. Grammar and direct grant schools were destroyed in order to abolish selection at eleven. Independent schools are threatened with closure for much the same reason – a policy document, *Labour's Programme 1982*, for example, outlines a ten year programme of abolition that includes a proposed parliamentary bill that 'would end subsidies to private schools and give the Education Secretary powers to forbid private schools charging fees for admissions' (quoted in *The TES*, 2 July 1982). Yet selection has reappeared within comprehensive schools. Setting, banding, and streaming are the direct means by which schools sort and sift their children by ability in diverse subjects. As we have seen in chapter 6, these practices are commonplace in British schools and are admitted to be such by supporters of comprehensive schooling – although deplored by them. There are some mixed-ability classes in the first and second years of (probably) about just over half our comprehensive schools. This form of organisation is adopted in most schools largely for diagnostic purposes to help in the selecting of pupils for setting in individual subjects, or for the complex option systems, organised in many schools for pupils from the age of fourteen. And there is evidence (see chapter 6) that most teachers distinguish between the 'most able', 'average', and 'least able' children within such mixed-ability classes; and that they generally teach 'towards the middle' – thus rejecting thereby the notion of 'individualised learning', accounted to be the secret of the difficult art of mixed-ability teaching.

In addition, some schools, such as Eltham Green, under headmaster Peter Dawson, provide remedial and compensatory education for the least intellectually able children in special units detached from the main school. Indeed, Dawson believes that 'There is no way of meeting the needs of the extremely slow learner without letting everyone know who he is.' (1981. p. 32.) Examinations for pupils at sixteen or eighteen years of age also necessitate grouping by ability. Few teachers believe that mixed-ability grouping can be used if pupils are preparing for examinations. Such a form of grouping is neither fair to those pupils sitting the examinations *or* those that are not. Although as we have seen this leads some supporters of comprehensive schooling to advocate the abolition of all examinations and their replacement by pupil 'profiles', this is not a view widely shared by teachers or parents.

The move to abolish selection, both between and within schools, did not have wide support from the general public, parents, or teachers. Indeed, Marsden in a Fabian Society pamphlet, *Politicians, equality and comprehensives*, pointed out that in the 1960s, 'Claims of a mandate for comprehensives was so much eyewash.' (1971, p. 14.) The abolition of selection as the goal of educational policy was pursued largely by the Labour Party – and, perhaps, only by a faction within it.[16] For many Labour supporters and local authorities 'such as those in Durham and South Wales were proud of the grammar schools they had built and which they had reserved entirely for the most able boys and girls regardless of social class' (Pedley, 1977, p. 8). And as Marsden wrote presciently in 1971, the shift in policy within the Labour Party, from support of a selective system to advocacy of comprehensive schooling, is 'for the majority of the party (a shift), merely from unequal educational provision in different schools to the provision of different and unequal education within the same school' (p. 4).

Comprehensive schools have failed also to increase the opportunities genuinely open to the children within them. As is widely agreed by supporters of comprehensive schools, such schools require to be large in order to provide curricular fare sufficiently nourishing for the considerable range of educational appetites within them. School statistics reveal, however, that comprehensives vary considerably in size – with a number considerably below what might be considered a viable size. Nor have comprehensive schools yet discovered how to cope with the differing curricular needs of their pupils. Most operate complex option schemes that lead to unbalanced programmes of study for many pupils, and are of such a complexity as to baffle the understanding of teachers, pupils, and parents. Such option schemes, however, do not guarantee that all combinations of options are available to all pupils – the HMIs' survey (1979) indeed suggests that the least able pupils may suffer under option schemes operated in some schools. In addition, option schemes create problems of movement about the school that may, in turn, have deleterious consequences for school discipline, and encourage truancy.

As an alternative to option schemes, some teachers and educationalists are advocating a common curriculum, to be followed in mixed ability classes by all pupils irrespective of their interests or aptitudes. Given that there are genuine differences of ability between children (a premise rarely denied by supporters of comprehensive schooling) such a programme is likely to penalise the least intellectually able – a number of whom can barely read or write on entry to secondary school. Such pupils struggle to make some sense of the flood of worksheets that descend upon them from teachers attempting to cope with pedagogic difficulties of mixed-ability teaching. The least able pupils may fail, thus, to have their particular needs satisfied, and will rapidly – and understandably – become bored with, and resentful of, all that school stands for. The common curricula will also, although this may be of little concern to some supporters of comprehensive schools, hold back the most able pupils, and will limit their access to studies they might profitably start at an early age. In these schools, scarce specialist staff will be spread thinly throughout the school – that is, if such staff have not left comprehensive schools for specialist posts in the sixth-form and tertiary colleges.

Nor has comprehensive reorganisation destroyed differences between schools located within a variety of catchment areas. Rutter, *et al*, for example, have indicated the differences that are to be found between ILEA comprehensive schools both in intake, as categorised by ability and ethnic origin, and in terms of the general ethos of the schools – their discipline and level of academic achievements (*Fifteen Thousand Hours*, 1979). Such differences between comprehensive schools can be justified as revealing diversity rather than inequality within the comprehensive school system. However, comprehensive school supporters suspect that diversity cloaks unjustifiable inequalities: as in the Labour Party policy document (see above) that would permit voluntary schools to admit pupils on denominational grounds – 'but not through testing or interviews employed as devices for selection on academic grounds' (quoted in *The TES*, 2 June 1982). Indeed Caroline Benn has questioned that 'selectivity which can result when a local authority decides to let some comprehensives specialise, while others do not'. An example Benn gives of such questionable specialisation is when, as one headteacher respondent to her survey noted, 'One form of entry is admitted each year of English-speaking pupils who are "good at Welsh". They are also likely to be good at maths, science, history, etc. This is obviously a selective intake.' (1976, p. 28.)

Have comprehensive schools improved the educational opportunities of the most able working class boys and girls? John Gray, in a contribution to *Education in the Eighties, the Central Issues*, in something of an understatement, remarks: 'In the short term . . . the effects of reorganisation on equalising educational opportunities remain unclear.' (1981, p. 89.) Gray indeed suggests that since comprehensive schools have 'decided to provide opportunities for many more of their children rather than "sponsoring" their most able, the "handicap" suffered by able working class children may well have been increased' (1981, p. 90). Whilst one may be sceptical of the claim that the loss to able working class children has been balanced by the gain in opportunities for more average children, the argument that comprehensives may be worsening the educational opportunities of able working class children is given support in Auriol Steven's statement: 'In 1974, 15 per cent of male applicants to Cambridge were the sons of manual workers, in 1979, 12 per cent. In this respect, comprehensives may not be helping.' (1980, p. 107.) In a response to the inadequacies of some comprehensive schooling, Oxford and Cambridge colleges are considering ways of reforming their admissions procedures. New procedures may permit candidates from comprehensive schools (particularly those sited in the 'inner-city') to be admitted with poorer qualifications than candidates from independent schools. However praiseworthy this form of positive or (reverse) discrimination may be, what an indictment of falling standards in comprehensive schools it constitutes!

Nor is there any evidence that comprehensive schools socially integrate children of differing social class, ethnic background, religious denomination, and sex. This is, in part, because even the necessary first step for social integration has not been taken: the creation of schools that constitute a microcosm of society. To create such schools, given the facts of social geography, would demand a degree of social engineering and political control as yet unacceptable to most people. The failure (for good or for ill) to distribute children from minority ethnic groups throughout British schools is evidence of this; as is the determination of the major Christian denominations to hang on to the control of what schools they see as their own – despite the fact that such schools are maintained largely from the public purse. The number of single-sex schools has, however, declined – perhaps because of the abolition of many single-sex grammar schools.

It is worth noting, in this context, that the abolition of all-girls grammar schools is likely to have reduced opportunities and incentives for intellectually able girls to do well at school – particularly in maths and sciences. Margaret Sutherland, Professor of Education at Leeds University, observes in her *Sex Bias in Education*: 'Coeducation has been expected to give equal opportunity, but in practice it seems to have increased sex differences in choice of subjects . . .', largely because of the workings of complex option systems in coeducational comprehensive schools. Sutherland adds: 'Academic ambitions may flourish more among girls at any rate, when competition with the opposite sex is not part of the learning situation.' (1981, p. 206.) Yet the determination of at least some supporters of comprehensive schools to ensure that such schools are compulsorily coeducational may be gauged by Daunt's assertion that 'Anyone who is convinced that single-sex education is a deprivation will wish to deny parents the right to inflict it on their children.' (1975, p. 71.)

Even in schools that, by chance rather than by management, achieve a tolerable 'social mix' there is little evidence that the school itself is a strong influence on how children view other social groups, or on the friends they choose. As do adults, children choose their friends for many reasons – including shared interests and outlooks. Sometimes, such common interests and outlooks overcome the solidarity of sex, ethnic group, and religious denomination; perhaps more often they do not. The impact of schools in this – despite their elaborate pastoral systems and trained counsellors – is probably very small. Supporters of comprehensive schools often argue that, in the last resort, such schools are justified in terms of establishing a more equal society. Have they come anywhere near achieving such an aim? Whether we define equality in terms of opportunity, outcome, or respect, the answer is 'no'. Indeed, it seems that at least some supporters of comprehensive schooling have lost their faith that schools can create a more equal society. For example, Professor Halsey argues that 'the geographical distribution of the social classes and the subtleties of the interaction between school and family . . . result in a continuing association of class origin with education destination' (1980, p. 73). And John Gunnell, writing on 'Education Policy' in *Labour into the Eighties*, points out: 'With 80 per cent of our children in comprehensives and apparently very little progress towards equality, it would be reasonable to question the system – especially as the secondary survey links success to catchment areas.' (1980, p. 93.) Yet despite the reasonableness of such doubts, Gunnell, a university lecturer in education, and in 1980, leader of the Labour group on the West Yorkshire Metropolitan County Council, could perversely argue that the Labour Party's manifesto, for a future general election, must contain the assertion: 'The completion of the comprehensive system must again be the top priority.' (p. 100.)

Perhaps we ought also to ask whether comprehensive schools have increased inequalities of outcome and opportunity. The evidence presented in this book at least suggests this is a possibility: a view given some support by John Gray who suggests that 'the abolition of the direct grant and grammar schools . . . may also, have *reduced* the chances for such working class children as would formerly have gained access to them' (1981, p. 90, my italics). In short, comprehensive schools have failed to fulfil the aims so confidently set for them by their advocates.

Nevertheless, this latter statement – and the whole of this chapter so far – contains little that many a committed supporter of comprehensive schooling would deny. For, as the reader will have surely noted by now, doubts about the reorganisation of secondary schools and the workings of the comprehensive system are expressed by its staunchest supporters. Some, like Denis Marsden and Caroline Benn, blame the politicians for the failure of the system – reserving their bitterest criticisms for those of their own party. Such critics can find much at fault with the secondary system of education they were so instrumental in creating, whilst never doubting the principle or theory of comprehensive schooling itself.

Indeed, logically there is a difference between ideal and reality. Ideals present us with desirable goals which, from the nature of the ideal, will never be completely realised – or else they would cease to serve as such. Thus, supporters of comprehensive organisation can argue that in this form of schooling we pursue an ideal, or constellation of ideals, which however hard we try, we will never be able to approach wholly in the practical, everyday world. From this point of view, present failure is only a spur to still further endeavour. The perceived present failure of comprehensive reorganisation to achieve its goals, they might say, does not discredit such schooling, it merely shows we have not been trying hard enough. And so more pressure groups must be formed, or jaded ones revitalised, to re-reorganise and re-group in pursuit of the will-o-the-wisp of the comprehensive ideal. If independent schools offend the 'law of coexistence', they must be abolished. If examinations delay the introduction of mixed ability classes, they must be abolished. If parental choice threatens the comprehensive system, that too must be abolished. If teachers remain obdurately conservative and reactionary in their outlook, they must be 'de-programmed' either in initial training, or through in-service courses. If able children threaten to develop more rapidly than their less able fellows, they must be relatively neglected to ensure that all march forward at the same pace. And if all fails – if the schools, however transformed, do not create the egalitarian utopia – the moral is 'that the comprehensive school must be part of a wider attack upon inequality' (Marsden, 1971, p. 18). A wider attack which must encompass who knows what targets.

Comprehensive schooling: the impossible dream?

However, it is my belief that the principle or theory of comprehensive schooling lacks coherence, and therefore cannot usefully serve as an ideal to be pursued by teachers, and other educational policy-makers. In part, this point is recognised and accepted – however obscurely – by some advocates of comprehensive schools. For instance Maurice Holt, in a book assuming 'that the comprehensive school should be seen, and increasingly is being seen, as the normal secondary school for all pupils', can nevertheless argue that 'The comprehensive school . . . took shape not from a clear educational vision, but from a political solution to the problem of pupil selection.' (1978, p. 19.) And although Holt accepts that there is no conclusive, widely convincing argument for comprehensive schools: 'Happily, though, the general drift is in the right direction' – towards comprehensive reorganisation (1978, p. 7).

The comprehensive principle is of little help in practice. It does not help determine how a comprehensive school should be organised, or what should be taught in it. By the 1960s it was clear that some important and influential supporters of comprehensive schooling, such as C. A. R. Crosland, thought it enough 'to avoid the extreme social division caused by physical segregation into schools of widely divergent status', after which: 'Division into streams according to ability remains essential.' (Crosland, 1956, p. 272.) Yet this latter notion was anathema to reformers such as Pedley and Benn, for whom selection within comprehensive schools is as unacceptable as selection between schools. Nevertheless, within this group, it is difficult to know whether selection can be welcomed at any stage within education. Pedley argues that comprehensive education does not stop at the end of compulsory schooling. Is selection by ability and aptitude, then, unacceptable for any course of training and education? There is no clear and unequivocal answer to this question.

A further difficulty arises from the fact that pupils for schools must be selected according to some criteria. If we abandon selection by ability and aptitude, what do we put in their place? Parental choice immediately suggests itself – but this is also rejected by the advocates of comprehensive schools, as leading to a state of affairs even more unfair and objectionable than that created by the now abolished eleven-plus. In practice, selection for schooling has come to be decided by politicians and administrators, who use catchment areas as the means of determining the intake of schools. This process, however, cannot guarantee that comprehensive schools are comprehensive in anything but name. Thus the negative (or comprehensive) principle does not take us far; it permits only the abolition of state schools whose intake were selected on the grounds of ability. (Although interestingly enough the 1976 Act specifically excluded special schools (for those with mental and other disabilities) and schools 'based on selection wholly or mainly by reference to ability or aptitude for music or dancing.')

If we turn to the more positive arguments for comprehensive schooling we find again division amongst its supporters. Comprehensive schooling is sometimes justified on the grounds that it provides equality of opportunity for all pupils. Yet much the same was said of the selective system it replaced. Of course, literally interpreted, equality of opportunity can never be achieved. Given differences in inherited capacities and abilities, differences in home and cultural background, and the diversity of opportunities open to individuals at one time and in one place, opportunities are not literally equal for all. Equality of opportunity makes more sense conceived of as 'open competition for scarce resources' (see Flew, 1981); the endeavour of teachers in applying this notion in the context of schooling is aimed at ensuring that only relevant criteria are employed in selecting pupils for courses. Perfection in this process is unlikely, yet as Gray points out, in the despised selective system: 'selectors selected those who were best qualified in terms of the established criteria, regardless of background' (1981, p. 85).

Not only may the principle of equality of opportunity be (and it was) used to justify selective education, it may also be employed to justify inequalities of attainment or outcome. For whilst we may open our schools and universities to those most capable of profiting by them, this cannot guarantee that all will make equal progress; indeed, rather the reverse. As is often remarked, equality of opportunity provides opportunities for inequality. For this reason, supporters of comprehensive education are uneasy with it – except as a useful and persuasive slogan. Inequalities of outcome in education are falsely seen as indicating a lack of open and competitive access to educational resources. For example, Halsey argues that egalitarians assume 'unless there is proof to the contrary, inequality of outcome in the social distribution of knowledge is a measure of *de facto* inequality of access' (1980, p. 57), no doubt in the spirit of assuming all accused persons, in this case those who select, to be guilty unless there is proof to the contrary.

Equality of opportunity as a principle of comprehensive schooling is, then, rejected by many supporters of such schooling on the grounds that it may be employed to justify selection by ability and aptitude within the school, and in support of the view that the school is an agent for the meritocratic society. P. E. Daunt (see chapter 2) in its place proposed the principle of equal worth. But, as I argued in chapter 2, when not high-sounding cant, such a principle is either a rephrasing of the principle of equality of opportunity, or a plea that we respect people *equally* – despite their differences in achievement, moral worth, etc. Indeed, this point is well put by Daunt's fellow headmaster, Maurice Holt who, in a comment on Daunt's guiding principle, remarks that 'it suffers from the disadvantage that it could, perversely, be used to justify a tripartite system by claiming that pupils meeting certain objective-test outcomes need a grammar school education' (1978, p. 24). And as yet a further step in defining the indefinable, Holt suggests that in place of Daunt's principle we put 'the notion of a common school offering a unified common culture' (1978, p. 24).

Advocates of comprehensive schooling attempt to reconcile the view that all children are different ('No two children are the same; that is a truism') with the belief that all children ought to be treated equally. Inevitably there is some equivocation over the meaning of 'equality'. On some occasions, it seems, a literally understood equality is the order of the day: with the consequence that all children, despite their differences, are to be treated and taught alike in mixed-ability classes following, as in Holt's suggestion, a common curriculum embodying 'a unified common culture'. This approach has the obvious disadvantage of ignoring the different needs, abilities, and aptitudes of children. Translated into practice, it presents the teacher with the impossible task of teaching his subject (however defined) to children of disparate capacities – with the results explored in chapter 6.

In yet other interpretations, 'equality' is not to be understood literally, but is a matter of teaching children in a way that pays attention to their individual interests and needs. 'Individualised learning' replaces class teaching. This reformed pedagogy, however, does not resolve the problem of equality, for the teacher still has to decide how much of his necessarily scarce time, attention, and resources, to devote to one child rather than another. Do the more backward claim most of his time? Or should he give the greatest attention to the most gifted in his class? An appeal to the principle of equality alone, or to notions such as 'need' and 'interest', do not help the teacher to come to a decision. In practice, in schools as they are, such individualised teaching is not workable. It is not surprising, then, that Marsden could summarise comprehensive theory as 'a tradition of thought stretching back to some idealised pre-industrial and pre-urban community, alongside a half-hearted and unpractical attempt at rational planning'. (1971, p. 31.)

Indeed Marsden's pamphlet drew attention to a marked division in the ranks of comprehensive school supporters. A division between those who supported comprehensive schooling because they believed it would more efficiently achieve the goals previously pursued within the selective system, and those who advocated such schools on the grounds that they would help create an egalitarian society. Marsden not only drew attention, thereby, to the differing views of comprehensive schooling amongst its supporters, but also (and perhaps inadvertently) to its incoherence as a doctrine. For it is difficult to have much faith in the intelligibility of an educational theory that can point to such widely different destinations. In a remarkable aside on the trends in opinions and attitudes which give support to comprehensive schooling, P. E. Daunt comments that what he is trying to describe 'can be thought of as adding up to something negative, as expressing nothing more than a loss of confidence and authority, a disintegration of values, coeval perhaps with a loss of mere power and energy in the West, a decadence therefore' (1975, p. 108).

Comprehensive schools, then, not only fail in practice; the theory on which they are based is incoherent and therefore can be no guide to practice. Failure arises not just from the reluctance of politicians to go all the way with such schooling. It arises more fundamentally from the lack of intelligibility of the doctrine itself, which is shot through with confusions and contradictions. Comprehensive schooling is thus 'the impossible dream'.

Postscript: where do we go from here?

I have set out in this book to review critically the theory and practice of comprehensive schooling in Britain. That task I have now completed. Readers may nevertheless wonder what may be done if the argument developed in this book is substantially correct. As Harold Macmillan is reputed once to have remarked: 'Here we are and where do we go from here?'

I suggest that as a necessary first step we must be as honest and truthful as we can about the present state of Britain's secondary schools. This is not easy or straightforward. Those that have laboured mightily to create the comprehensive system take up different attitudes to their creature. Some continue to find much fault with it – pointing out the degree to which it fails to match up to the comprehensive ideal. This group contains perceptive critics of comprehensive schooling who are aware of its many defects. Unfortunately, they refuse to see the many deficiencies of comprehensive schools as evidence for the failure of the theory as such. This group acknowledges the many faults of comprehensive schooling, but these faults are supposed to be remedied by more such schooling, not less. For example, *Labour's Programme 1982*, proposes that a future Labour government would 'encourage the phasing out of streaming, particularly in the first years of secondary schools' (quoted in *The TES*, 2 July 1982). The further development of comprehensive schooling along these lines leads to the control of schools, their organisation and curricula, becoming more and more the direct and immediate responsibility of the LEAs and the state. Clearly, private schooling and parental choice are wholly incompatible with this vision of the comprehensive school.

Other supporters of comprehensive schooling refuse to see its imperfections; and indeed, they grasp at any indications, or research findings, that suggest all is well – or at least that comprehensive schooling may be no worse than the selective system it replaced. Such supporters are, however, thankfully unwilling to abolish private schooling, or to increase the scope of LEA or state control over the schools. As the comprehensive system is now the official and accepted system it receives the support that follows from this fact. Educational administrators and senior teachers are thus loath – at least in public – to criticise the system in which they work. It smacks too much of sawing off the branch while sitting on it. In addition, such criticism would lessen public confidence in the schools, which is not helpful to them, or conducive to that political support so necessary to institutions paid for out of the public purse.

Yet another group, made up of teachers in schools, are well aware of the deficiencies and inadequacies. These teachers have become sceptical of the virtues of comprehensive reorganisation through personal experience of it. Clyde Chitty, an editor of *Comprehensive Education*, has learnt from his teaching in comprehensive schools that 'many teachers are bewildered and sceptical' (1980, p. 153). He points out that 'those teachers who feel threatened by what they would regard as dangerous experimentation cannot all be written off as incompetent backwoodsmen who refuse to see the light' (Chitty, 1980, p. 153). Chitty's eleven years spent teaching in London comprehensives have taught him that there are 'a large number of dedicated professionals who were passionate in their defence of homogeneous groupings and at the same time had a genuine concern for all the children they taught' (1980, p. 153). However, such 'dedicated professionals' may find it prudent to keep their doubts to themselves – or air them within the relative privacy of their staffrooms. For a number of LEAs confuse loyalty to schools, and concern for the children within them, with uncritical acceptance of the system of secondary education they have established.

Indeed some LEAs demand a kind of comprehensive 'loyalty oath' from their teachers, whereby promotion within comprehensive schools must be accompanied by a public declaration of allegiance to the comprehensive principle.[16] Such measures do not encourage an honest evaluation of comprehensive schooling.

Educational researchers and research organisations could play an important part in an honest appraisal of our school system. Although the social sciences cannot match up to the standards of objectivity and experimentation in the natural sciences, this does not mean that they can abandon the quest for whatever standard of fact-neutrality they can achieve. The essence of scientific methodology is looking for counter-evidence, not seeking that which all too easily comes to hand: confirmation of one's precious theories and hypotheses. Unfortunately, in practice, all too often researchers are employed to give spurious scientific support to untested social and educational theories. And sometimes researchers themselves connive only too willingly in this dubious enterprise. Nevertheless, comprehensive theory and practice could be tested by looking for counter-evidence for some of its theses – for example, in considering such questions as: to what extent do students in tertiary colleges become socially and intellectually integrated?

I suggest also that honesty about our social institutions becomes more difficult the greater the degree they are controlled by the state. It is more difficult to challenge 'official truths' precisely because they have the backing of the state: and a state monstrously swollen by its incorporation of major social institutions such as schooling and education. Supporters of comprehensive schooling believe, quite rightly, that such a system can only be established by the employment of state power directed from the centre. Only by such means can the desired uniformity of schooling be achieved. Of course, all these efforts are doomed to failure because even the most powerful state has yet to gain control of family life: so potent an influence on inequalities. Nevertheless, the expression of rational and reasonable criticism of compulsory comprehensivisation becomes ever more difficult under such circumstances.

Therefore, policies that lead to a relaxation of state control over education require development. State control over education arises, largely, from our methods of financing schooling. The maintained (or state) schools are just that; they are maintained out of rates and taxes. How much is spent on schools, relative to other services in the welfare state, therefore rests with politicians and administrators. As such politicians are elected representatives, they often assume they are 'mandated' to pursue various policies which express the popular will. This assumption is largely mistaken, as witness the gap between the policy of comprehensive reorganisation pursued by local and national politicians, and the genuine grassroot support amongst the electorate for such a policy ('Claims of a mandate for comprehensives was so much eyewash' D. Marsden 1971, p. 14). However, so long as schools are funded out of the public purse, our elected representatives will continue, quite rightly, to control how such funds are disbursed. Means must be sought to return to parents and students the opportunity to pay directly (in whole and in part) for schooling. This is not a policy contrary to egalitarianism. There is now plenty of evidence that the welfare state, far from reducing inequalities of income and status, increases them. Le Grand, for example, in his *The Strategy of Equality* points out, in a summary of statistical evidence on the relationships between diverse social groups, public expenditure, and education: 'Overall it seems that public expenditure has failed as a means of achieving equality.' (1982, p. 77.) What, then, is required is more study and development of voucher and loan schemes that will both help to create some greater degree of choice for parents and students, and will reduce subsidies to those who can well afford to pay for at least a portion of the schooling they or their children receive.

In addition, any attempt to destroy private schooling must be strongly resisted. Such resistance is in the interests of those that would neither wish nor could afford to send their children to independent schools. For the destruction of private schooling would turn near-monopolistic state schooling into an absolute monopoly. And as Brenda Cohen points out, 'Without the existence of the independent yardstick, the temptation to argue that what people are getting is what they want may be even greater than it is.' (1981, p. 24.) The minimum policy to be followed is non-interference in private schooling. Indeed, possibly such schools should be given positive encouragement in terms of tax relief and exemptions. Individuals and commercial concerns could be encouraged to provide charitable gifts to improve the facilities of such schools, and to provide scholarships for poor scholars. In this way, opportunities for access to private schools will be increased. If reformers wish to lessen what they conceive to be the elite character of such schools and their 'social divisiveness', the answer is to help the schools to open their doors to more pupils – to make them more popular and less 'elitist'.

The state schools present a diversity of problems for the policy-maker. First, they have been subject to so many reorganisations in the last two decades, that one can respect those teachers who cry 'enough is enough'. And yet, as we have observed, the dynamic of comprehensive reorganisation permits no rest. The pursuit of equality has no final resting point – as the present reorganisation of the schools' sixth forms demonstrates. Every reorganisation creates fresh inequalities that have to be remedied by further reorganisation, *ad infinitum*. This process will only cease when we recognise that the goal of absolute equality is one not worth aiming at.

Let us take the example of the reorganisation of sixth forms. As I argued in chapter 7, it is now widely recognised that all schools cannot maintain a reasonably sized sixth form. For those whose unreasonable aim in educational policy is absolute equality, the answer, to the dilemma created by the presence in an LEA of schools with sixth forms alongside secondary schools without, is easy enough. If all schools cannot have sixth forms, the principle of absolute or flat equality demands that none shall. And yet who gains and who loses?

Let us admit that an 11–18 comprehensive school is better than an 11–16 school; it is likely to have greater status in the community, more specialist staff, and a wider curriculum. Pupils and teachers at the 11–16 school are in, as will surely be ruthlessly pointed out by the egalitarians in our midst, a second-class school. Pupils from such a school will have to join the sixth form of the 11–18 school if they wish to pursue sixth-form studies. (Yet it is worth noting, that the numbers of such pupils will be relatively small as otherwise the 11–16 school could sustain a sixth form.) But what will the 11–16 school gain if its neighbour also loses its sixth form? Its pupils will still have to leave school for post-compulsory schooling. The only satisfaction to be gained is the knowledge that all schools will now be second rated: a triumph of petty-minded envy?

On the other hand, teachers, pupils, and parents, in the 11–18 school, will have lost a great deal by the destruction of the sixth form of the school. Views of the virtues of school sixth forms vary; but there is at least opinion expressed that older pupils are useful, in general, to a school, and that such pupils may learn something of value in being junior leaders in their own schools – this may help in the development of maturity and confidence.

In addition, the upheaval following the reorganisation necessary to schools losing their sixth forms is likely to lead to some loss of morale among teachers: particularly as many of them value highly the sixth-form teaching they do. If those teachers, most qualified and able to teach sixth-form pupils, are encouraged to leave so as to form the nucleus of staff for the newly-created sixth-form college, there is a further loss to the school. A school which has lost its sixth form may thus be poorer in a number of ways than can be strictly calculated in terms of staff and pupil numbers. And while the pupils and staff of a school with a sixth form will be worse off after losing it, in what ways have the opportunities of 11–16 schools improved? All children will be treated more equally following reorganisation, but those least advantaged before, will not have much greater advantage after the change, whilst those children who were attending schools with sixth forms may be a good deal worse off.

Local authorities must frankly recognise that their comprehensive schools vary. If it is true, as Professor Briault claims, that 'few authorities appear to know what changes of this kind [in the intellectual ability of intake], if any, are happening' (1980, p. 79), then this is a scandal. LEAs ought to know the range of ability and attainments to be found in their schools. This is as true for the supporter of comprehensive schooling as its opponent – for how can an LEA know whether its comprehensive policy is successful or not unless it has information of this kind? We must know what many experienced observers suspect: that comprehensive schools are becoming divided into those comparable to former grammar schools and those that remain little different from the secondary moderns they replaced. *Plus ca change. . . .*

How we respond to the fact of comprehensive inequalities is a major policy question. Attempting to compulsorily equalise such schools has not worked, and will continue not to work in British society. (It fails to work in the Soviet Union so it is even less likely to work in Britain.) Let us then accept and acknowledge such inequalities between schools. As far as possible we can ensure that the most intellectually able, despite ethnic origin, social class, or neighbourhood, attend those schools that provide demanding studies which they can pursue alongside their intellectual peers. The needs of more average children can then be satisfied in schools in which they are in a majority. And, indeed, in such schools the least able children can be given that care and concern which will enable them to achieve at least the minimum standards of intellectual competence demanded in a modern society. This proposal will be described as a return to the former selective system by the front door. So be it, for we have seen how its alternative has failed nearly a generation of pupils. Nevertheless, we must learn from the destruction of the selective system and the failure of its replacement. The selective system was vulnerable; the neglect of some average and below average children in some secondary modern schools (as revealed in the Newsom Report (1963)) must not be repeated, however our comprehensive system evolves. But we cannot afford to neglect our most able children, whatever their social background, and leave them to waste their time and energies in mixed ability classes in schools desperately coping with the needs and interests of children differing widely in abilities and aptitudes.

Within our secondary schools, we must resist the doctrinaire demand that all classes ought to be mixed ability, for 'there is no one best way of organising pupils for all purposes' (Reid, 1981, p. 146). Indeed, if we value schools in terms of their teaching useful, practical, intellectual, and sporting skills, most classes will, *per force*, be homogeneous in character. (But, of course, it is equally dogmatic to demand that all of them are.) And despite the presence in some schools of authoritarian headteachers only too eager to pursue their libertarian and egalitarian policies despite the reservations and hostility of their staffs, the position of headteachers in schools requires to be safeguarded. In some respects (not all) the task of the head in the school resembles that of the captain of a ship; he must both set the school on a steady course and deal with unexpected emergencies. If we increase the powers of the governing bodies of schools and of schools councils within them, the authority and power of heads decline – the consequences of which may not be to the advantage of the schools. Of course, heads may abuse their powers, but so also may governing bodies and schools councils.

To conclude, we can expect two things from our schools: first, that they provide an adequate schooling for everyone – so that no one need leave school unable to read, write and count. If anyone considers that an absurdly minimum requirement, it must be said that a number of school leavers finish their schooling not yet able to read or write. And second, whilst we firmly plank down a floor beneath which no one will fall, we must encourage the fullest development of all those that are capable of a high level of achievement in those skills and subjects that schools can teach. And this is no impossible dream.

Notes

1 Such doubts were permitted a careful official expression in the 'Great Debate', initiated by Prime Minister Jim Callaghan in his speech at Ruskin College, Oxford, 18 October 1976. The Green Paper, in summarising the main points of this debate, noted that: 'The speech was made against a background of strongly critical comment in the press and elsewhere on education and educational standards.' (DES, 1977, p. 2.)

2 An influential study of this kind was *Social Class and Educational Opportunity* by J. E. Floud, A. H. Halsey, and F. M. Martin (London: Heinemann, 1956). Dr A. H. Halsey was later to become an important member of the 'educational establishment' of the 1960s and 1970s.

3 Opening sentence (p. 13) to his article 'Education and Equality' in *New Society*, 17 June 1965.

4 For a survey of the variety of procedures used by LEAs to allocate pupils to secondary schools, 1971/72, see C. J. Hill's *Transfer at Eleven* (Windsor: NFER, 1972).

5 A public opinion poll, commissioned by the Labour Party in 1957, revealed that only 10 per cent of the sample considered 'segregated' education to be socially undesirable.

6 Said in a TV programme in the pre-election period of 1964. It says a lot for the character of election promises that Sir Harold Wilson is in 1982 alive and well and representing the Labour interest in the House of Commons.

7 I owe this observation to Caroline Cox and John Marks who, in their pamphlet *Real Concern* (1981), claim that the interpretation of the findings of the NCDS (1980) by its own authors is strongly biased in favour of comprehensive schooling.

8 In 1971, when the Open University opened, Naomi McIntosh, its then Head of Survey Research Department, noted that teachers 'dominated our first year' (1974, p. 55). Indeed the OU encouraged such domination by providing 'credit exemptions' – thus shortening the time and effort required to graduate – for teachers, provided that they followed courses within the OU's Faculty of Educational Studies.

9 C. A. R. Crosland also noted this paradox, and argued that it would 'be absurd from a socialist point of view to close down the grammar schools, while leaving the public schools still holding their present commanding position' (1956, p. 275). Yet when in office, Crosland perpetuated this absurdity.

10 The Taylor Report, *A New Partnership for Our Schools* (London: HMSO, 1977), recommended more parental and community representation on schools' governing bodies, and an increase in their powers. Some of these recommendations have been incorporated in the 1980 Education Act, but the all important increase in the powers of such bodies has proved unacceptable to the DES, LEAs, and teachers' unions.

11 Indeed *The Sunday Times* gave as an example: 'The head of a London boy's comprehensive, whose own two boys, aged 12 and 14, attend independent day schools. He feels that public schools offer more chance of examination passes "because of (a) academic environment and (b) social environment". He would have chosen a state school instead if there had been "a higher percentage of well-adjusted, well-motivated children of good academic calibre in the state schools – but they are not around in such numbers any more in inner London".'

12 In pre-war years, the Spens Report on secondary education with special reference to grammar schools and technical high schools, argued that as the size of multilateral schools 'would have to be considerable, say 800 or possibly larger', there was much to be said for the then *status quo* (1938, p. xx).

13 Professor Halsey has been an important and influential member of the 'educational establishment' identified by Professor Maurice Kogan (1971, p. 46).

14 See Chart 3.14, p. 51, in *Social Trends 12* (1981).

15 It is interesting to note that Joan Sallis represented the interests of parents on the Taylor Committee, later to produce the report, *A New Partnership for Our Schools* (London: HMSO, 1977).

16 A Labour Party policy document, *Labour's Programme 1982*, now recognises that defining comprehensive schools as 'non-selective' is 'insufficiently positive'. Instead the approved definition may well become: 'a system in which all children

have the right to experience a broadly based curriculum, with equal access to all the opportunities offered in a school – regardless of attainment or sex – with due emphasis upon the multi-cultural nature of British society' (quoted in *The TES*, 2 July 1982). *The Daily Telegraph's* Peter Simple could not have done better.

Bibliography

Ashby, P. 'Comprehensive Post-School Education' in Rubinstein D. (Ed.) *Education and Equality* (London: Harper and Row, 1980)

Batley, R. O'Brien, O. and Parris, A. *Going Comprehensive* (London: Routledge and Kegan Paul, 1970)

Belski, R. 'Ideology and the Comprehensive Schools' in *Political Quarterly*, No. 44, 1973

Benn, C. *Comprehensive or Coexistence – 'We must choose which we want'* (London: National Union of Teachers, 1976)

Benn, C. and Simon, B. *Half Way There* (London: McGraw-Hill, 1970)

Boyd, D. *Elites and their Education* (Windsor: NFER, 1973)

Briault, E. and Smith, F. *Falling Rolls in Secondary Schools*, Part One (Windsor: NFER, 1980)

Brook, L. 'Sixteen to nineteen equals minus one million – right?' in Rubinstein, D. (Ed.) *Education and Equality* (London: Harper and Row, 1980)

Bullivant, B. 'Parental Choice and its Dangers' in *Comprehensive Education* No. 37, Winter 1977/78

Burgess, T. *Inside Comprehensive Schools* (London: HMSO, 1970)

Cantor, L. M. and Roberts, I. F. *Further Education Today: A Critical Review* (London: Routledge and Kegan Paul, 1979)

Chitty, C. 'Inside the Secondary School: Problems and Prospects' in Rubinstein, D. (Ed.) *Education and Equality* (London: Harper and Row, 1980)

Chitty, C. 'Why Comprehensive Schools?' in *Forum* Vol. 24(1) Autumn 1981

Cohen, B. *Education and the Individual* (London: Allen and Unwin, 1981)

Cooper, D. *Illusions of Equality* (London: Routledge and Kegan Paul, 1980)

Cox, C. and Marks, J. *Real Concern* (London: Centre for Policy Studies, 1981)

Crosland, C. A. R. *The Future of Socialism* (London: Jonathan Cape, 1956)
Crowther Report, Ministry of Education, *15 to 18*, Vol. 1, Report (London: HMSO, 1959)

Daunt, P. E. *Comprehensive Values* (London: Heinemann Educational Books, 1975)
Davis, R. *The Grammar School* (Harmondsworth: Penguin, 1967)
Dawson, P. *Making a comprehensive work: the road from Bomb Alley* (Oxford: Basil Blackwell, 1981)
Dennison, W. F. *Education in Jeopardy: Problems and Possibilities of Contraction* (Oxford: Basil Blackwell, 1981)
Department of Education and Science, *Aspects of secondary education in England. A survey by HM Inspectors of Schools* (London: HMSO, 1979)
Department of Education and Science, *Education in Schools: A Consultative Document* (London: HMSO, 1977)
Department of Education and Science, *Circular 10/65: The Organisation of Secondary Education* (London: HMSO, 1965)
Department of Education and Science, 'Patterns of Secondary Organisation' (HMI Paper) in *Aspects of Comprehensive Education* (London: DES, 1978)
Department of Education and Science, *Statistics of Education, 1979, Schools*, Vol. 1 (London: HMSO, 1981)
Donnison, D. V. 'Education and Opinion' in *New Society* (No. 256) 26 Oct. 1967
Donnison Report, Second Report of the Public Schools Commission, Vol 1: *Report on Independent Day Schools and Direct Grant Grammar Schools* (London: HMSO, 1970)
Douglas, J. W. B. 'The use and abuse of National Cohorts' in Shipman, M. (Ed.) *The Organisation and Impact of Social Research* (London: Routledge and Kegan Paul, 1976)

Education Group (Centre for Contemporary Cultural Studies) *Unpopular Education, Schooling and Social Democracy in England Since 1944* (London: Hutchinson, 1981)

Fenwick, I. G. K. *The Comprehensive School, 1944–1970: the politics of secondary school reorganisation* (London: Methuen, 1976)
Flew, A. *The Politics of Procrustes. Contradictions of enforced equality* (London: Temple Smith, 1981)
Ford, J. *Social Class and the Comprehensive School* (London: Routledge and Kegan Paul, 1969)

Grace, G. *Teachers, Ideology and Control: A Study in Urban Education* (London: Routledge and Kegan Paul, 1978)
Gray, J. 'From policy to practice – some problems and paradoxes of egalitarian reform', in Simon, B. and Taylor, W. (Ed.) *Education in the Eighties, the Central Issues* (London: Batsford, 1981)
Gunnell, J. 'Education Policy' in Bell, D. S. (Ed.) *Labour into the Eighties* (London: Croom Helm, 1980)

Halsall, E. *The Comprehensive School, Guidelines for the Reorganisation of Secondary Education* (Oxford: Pergamon Press, 1973)

Halsey, A. H. 'Social Mobility and Education' in Rubinstein, D. (Ed.) *Education and Equality* (London: Harper and Row, 1980)

Hargreaves, D. H. *The Challenge for the Comprehensive School: Culture, Curriculum and Community* (London: Routledge and Kegan Paul, 1982)

Hayek, F. A. *The Mirage of Social Justice*, Vol. 2 (Chicago: The University of Chicago Press, 1976)

Hearnshaw, L. S. *Cyril Burt: psychologist* (London: Hodder and Stoughton, 1979)

Hinton, M. *Comprehensive schools: a Christian's view* (London: SCM Press, 1979)

Holt, M. *The Common Curriculum, its Structure and Style in the Comprehensive school* (London: Routledge and Kegan Paul, 1978)

Husén, T. *The School in Question* (Oxford University Press, 1979)

Jackson, B. and Marsden, D. *Education and the Working Class* (London: Routledge and Kegan Paul, 1962)

James, P. H. *The Reorganization of Secondary Education* (Windsor: NFER, 1980)

Kirp, D. L. *Doing Good by Doing Little: Race and Schooling in Britain* (Berkeley: University of California Press, 1979)

Kogan, M. with Boyle, E. and Crosland C. A. R. *The Politics of Education* (Harmondsworth: Penguin, 1971)

Kogan, M. *et al, County Hall, The Role of the Chief Education Officer* (Harmondsworth: Penguin, 1973)

Kogan, M. *The Politics of Educational Change* (London: Fontana, 1978)

Le Grand, J. *The Strategy of Equality, Redistribution and the Social Services* (London: Allen and Unwin, 1982)

Macfarlane Review, Department of Education and Science, *Education for 16–19 year olds: a review undertaken for the Government and the Local Authority Associations* (London: HMSO, 1981)

Maclure, J. Stuart (Ed.) *Educational Documents: England and Wales* (London: Methuen, 1973)

McIntosh, N. 'The OU Student' in Tunstall, J. (Ed.) *The Open University Opens.* (London: Routledge and Kegan Paul, 1974)

Makins, V. 'Countesthorpe College – the First Five Years' in Watts J. (Ed.) *The Countesthorpe Experience* (London: George Allen and Unwin, 1977)

Marsden, D. 'Which Comprehensive Principle?' in *Comprehensive Education*, No. 13 Autumn 1969

Marsden, D. *Politicians, Equality and Comprehensives* (London: Fabian Society, 1971)

Midwinter, E. *Priority Education: An Account of the Liverpool Project* (Harmondsworth: Penguin, 1972)

Midwinter, E. 'Teachers' centres: The facilitators' in *British Journal of Inservice Education*, Vol. 1 (1) 1974

Naylor, F. *Crisis in The Sixth Form* (London: Centre for Policy Studies, 1981)

Newsom Report, *Half Our Future* (London: HMSO, 1963)

Newsom Report, *First Report of the Public Schools Commission, Vol. 1: Report* (London: HMSO, 1968)

NFER, *Local Authority Practices in the Allocation of Pupils to Secondary Schools* (Windsor: NFER, 1964)

NOP, Gretton, J. *Teachers in the British General Election of October 1974 (Report of a survey carried out by NOP on behalf of The Times Educational Supplement and The Times Higher Education Supplement)* (London: Times Newspapers, 1975)

Parkinson, M. *The Labour Party and the Organisation of Secondary Education 1918–1965* (London: Routledge and Kegan Paul, 1970)

Patterson, C. H. 'The Selection of Counsellors' in Whitely, J. M. (Ed.) *Research in Counselling* (Ohio: Merrill, 1968)

Pedley, R. *Towards the Comprehensive University* (London: Macmillan, 1977)

Pedley, R. *The Comprehensive School* (Harmondsworth: Penguin, 1978)

Peters, R. S. *Ethics and Education* (London: George Allen and Unwin, 2nd ed. 1970)

Rae, J. *The Public School Revolution: Britain's Independent Schools, 1964–1979* (London: Faber and Faber, 1981)

Ravitch, D. *The Revisionists Revised* (New York: Basic Books, 1978)

Rée, H. *The Essential Grammar School* (London: Harrap, 1956)

Reid, M. I., *et al, Mixed Ability Teaching: Problems and Possibilities* (Windsor: NFER, 1981)

Ribbins, P. M. and Brown, R. J. 'Policy Making in English Local Government: The Case of Secondary School Reorganisation' in *Public Administration*, No. 57, 1979

Rubinstein, D. and Simon, B. *The Evolution of the Comprehensive School, 1926–1972* (London: Routledge and Kegan Paul, 1973)

Rutter, M., *et al, Fifteen Thousand Hours: Secondary Schools and their effects on children* (London: Open Books, 1979)

Saran, R. *Policy-making in Secondary Education* (Oxford University Press, 1973)

Silver, H. *Equal Opportunity in Education* (London: Methuen, 1973)

Simon, B. 'The Neighbourhood School' in *Comprehensive Education* No. 4, Autumn 1966

Simon, B. 'Countesthorpe in the Context of Comprehensive Development' in Watts, J. (Ed.) *The Countesthorpe Experience* (London: George Allen and Unwin, 1979)

Simon, Lady, of Wythenshawe *Three Schools or One? Secondary education in England, Scotland and the USA* (London: Frederick Muller, 1948)

Sharp, J. *Open School. The experience of 1964–1970 at Wyndham School, Egremont, Cumberland* (London: Dent, 1973)

Skrimshire, A. 'Community Schools and the Education of the "Social Individual"' in *Oxford Review of Education* 7 (1) 1981

Social Trends 12 (London: HMSO, 1981)

Spens Report, Board of Education, *Report of the Consultative Committee on Secondary Education, with Special Reference to Grammar Schools and Technical High Schools* (London: HMSO, 1938)

Steedman, J. *Progress in Secondary Schools: Findings from the National Child Development Study* (London: National Children's Bureau, 1980)

Steedman, J. and Fogelman, K. 'Secondary Schooling: Findings from the National Child Development Study' in *Concern*, No. 36, Summer 1980

Stevens, A. *Clever Children in Comprehensive Schools* (Harmondsworth: Penguin, 1980)

Storm, M. 'Profile: Countesthorpe College' in *Where*, No. 79, April 1973

Sutherland, M. *Sex Bias in Education* (Oxford: Basil Blackwell, 1981)

Taylor, G. 'Comprehensive inequalities' in *New Society*, 1st July 1965

Taylor, G. and Saunders, J. B. *The Law of Education, First Supplement to Eighth Edition* (London: Butterworths, 1980)

Taylor, M. and Garson Y. 'Too Great Expectations?' in *The TES*, 26 March 1982

Taylor, M. and Garson, Y. *Schooling for the Middle Years* (Trentham: Trentham Books, 1982)

Tawney, R. H. *Equality* (London: Allen and Unwin, rev. ed. 1952)

Tawney, R. H. (Ed.) *Secondary Education for All: A Policy for Labour* (London: Allen and Unwin, 1922)

The Sunday Times, 'Why Parents choose Private Schools', 28 February, 1982

Vaughan, T. *Education and the Aims of Counselling, a European Perspective* (Oxford: Basil Blackwell, 1975)

Vernon, B. D. *Ellen Wilkinson 1891–1947* (London: Croom Helm, 1982)

Warnock, M. *Schools of Thought* (London: Faber and Faber, 1977)

Warnock, M. *Education: a way ahead* (Oxford: Basil Blackwell, 1979)

Waters, R. 'Teachers for Comprehensive Education' in *Forum*, 13 (1) Autumn 1970

Watts, J. 'An Address to Parents, 19th June, 1974' in Watts, J. (Ed.) *The Countesthorpe Experience* (London: George Allen and Unwin, 1977)

Watts, J. *Towards an Open School* (London: Longman, 1980)

Weston, P. B. *Framework for the Curriculum* (Windsor: NFER, 1977)

Williams, S. *Politics is for People* (Harmondsworth: Penguin, 1981)

White, J. P. 'Tyndale and the Left' in *Forum*, Vol. 19 (2) Spring 1977

Wright, N. *Progress in Education: A Review of Schooling in England and Wales* (London: Croom Helm, 1977)

Young, M. and Willmott, P. *Family and Kinship in East London* (London: Routledge and Kegan Paul, 1957)

Young, M. F. D. 'An approach to the study of curricula as socially organised knowledge' in Young, M. F. D. (Ed.) *Knowledge and Control: New Directions for the Sociology of Education* (London: Collier–Macmillan, 1971)

Index